CHOW

CHOW

SIMPLE WAYS TO SHARE THE FOODS YOU LOVE
WITH THE DOGS YOU LOVE

RICK WOODFORD

The Countryman Press
A division of W. W. Norton & Company
Independent Publishers Since 1923

TO RALEIGH

One Quarter Dog,

One Quarter Girl,

One Quarter Boy,

One Quarter Squirrel.

CONTENTS

INTRODUCTION

As pet owners, we are fortunate to be in charge of the refrigerator and pantry. Every day we can choose from hundreds of favorite foods; sometimes those food choices are healthy and other times they fulfill a hankering for something tasty. Down on the floor, our four-legged family members salivate and wait for a share and we say, "No, this isn't for you." Instead our dogs eat the same food day after day because we're told to never give dogs "people food."

Thousands of years ago, dogs began walking beside us because we offered a source of food, shelter, adventure, and friendship. Today we provide our dogs with daily walks or a day at dog day care, comfortable beds (or couches) to sleep on, and, in some cases, jackets and sweaters to keep them warm and dry. Unfortunately, when it comes to food, we've outsourced our responsibility in caring for our pets. In exchange for convenience, our pets are living shorter lives, requiring more medical care, and carrying excess weight.

With half of our dogs developing cancer today, the question has to be asked, "What are we doing wrong?" It's not that commercial foods are necessarily causing cancer; they simply cannot do enough to prevent it. What's missing? Fresh food filled with enzymes, antioxidants, wholesome protein, less carbohydrates, and natural vitamins and minerals rather than synthetic versions. Just as we've opened our hearts to dogs, it's time we opened our refrigerators as well.

We've all been warned by the pet food industry and our veterinarians to never alter our dogs' diet and to beware of upsetting the balance of nutrition in commercial pet foods. But there is room in the bowl for fresh foods. This book will make it easy for you, with simple, quick recipes using the foods you already incorporate into your own meals.

Each food in this book has multiple reasons to share it with your dog; collectively they aim to provide variety, nutrition unrepresented in the commercial foods, and convenience for you while lengthening the years you spend with your faithful companion. The bonus for your dog is new flavors, real nutrition to protect your pet's health, and generous serving sizes.

Real food makes the best *CHOW*!

Fresh foods contain around nine times the moisture of dry foods. The water content is calorie-free volume, allowing a larger portion size and lower calorie count than calorie-dense commercial dry foods. Don't be afraid of the portion sizes; the recipes include serving sizes that you can match to both the weight and energy level of your pet. Most active dogs fall right smack dab in the middle of the serving size listed which covers the range of inactive to extra active dogs.

FILLING THE EMPTY BOWL

As part of my effort to better understand canine nutrition, I went out to pet food companies and asked them for detailed nutritional breakdowns of their foods. Being a former dog food manufacturer myself, I was already familiar with the nutritional minimums from the Association of American Feed Control Officials (AAFCO)—a.k.a. the pet food industry—but knew there was another standard set by the independent National Research Council (NRC) that includes not just minimums, but recommended daily allowances. The NRC's standard defines not what your pet can survive on, but what your pet can thrive on. The NRC's recommendations are what I follow, and I wanted to see how other manufacturers measured up.

I surveyed 200 foods and compared them to the NRC standard. It's a lot of math, but I'm a nerd. The results were surprising and led me to believe that the "complete and balanced" formula referred to so often by pet food companies and veterinarians is often incomplete. The most surprising discovery was that there is no reason to fear fresh food; there's more than enough room in the bowl for natural sources of proteins, fats, vitamins, minerals, and antioxidants.

For pet foods to be truly complete, they should represent everything that your dog needs to be healthy. The absence of an omega-3 fatty acids requirement is only the beginning. The NRC's research clearly explains how these fats help with neurological development, improve overall health, and reduce inflammation. And omega-3s fight cancer. The AAFCO says, "Eh, dogs can do without them." Your dog's body and I do not agree.

Given that there are thousands of antioxidants in fresh food, I wouldn't expect every antioxidant to be represented. Some of those required by industry standards—such as vitamins A, C, E, and K—pull double duty as antioxidant and vitamin, while selenium is both a mineral and antioxidant. Vitamins C and E are also used because they're preservatives. Some of the most powerful antioxidants, though, are left out of the bag. "Eh, dogs can do without them." With 50 percent of dogs today diagnosed with cancer, I disagree and so does the body of the dogs with cancer. Anti-oxidants are drawn to different parts of the body and perform very different functions. Instead of gambling on a few antioxidants to protect every function in a dog's body, I prefer to hedge my bets with a wide variety of antioxidants from a wide variety of foods.

Except for a few cases, the foods I researched met both the NRC and the AAFCO minimum by 200 to 600 percent for most nutrients. Cut that in half and it's 100 to 300 percent. Even if only half of your dog's diet is from commercial food, it will meet your dog's requirement and leave room for fresh foods with quality protein, healthy fats, vitamins, minerals, and antioxidants. You won't upset the apple cart by giving your dog an apple, an egg, fish, or other healthy foods—you'll only be adding food that adds to your dog's long-term health.

The word *balance* should indicate precision and equilibrium of nutrients. But when it pertains to commercial pet foods, it doesn't. There are wide opinions about what it means to be balanced. Once manufacturers reach the minimum ratio of certain nutrients, they have a wildly different view on how nutrients should be met. There is no precise formula that all manufacturers are following and not everything your dog needs to truly remain healthy is represented in commercial foods. What commercial foods do have going for them, is that even as half of your dog's diet, the requirements for a narrow set of proteins, vitamins, and minerals will be met.

To meet what's missing . . . let's fill the bowl with fresh food.

In some cases additional supplementation may be necessary:

🐾 If you are adding only a modest amount of fresh foods to your dog's diet, there's no reason to supplement already highly supplemented commercial foods. If your veterinarian recommends an additional daily vitamin or mineral supplement, ask which specific nutrients are necessary. It's better to provide the individual nutrients rather than another high dose of every vitamin and mineral.

🐾 If less than 50 percent of your dog's overall diet is homemade, supplementation is optional because commercial foods are already supplemented between 200 and 600 percent of what your dog needs. If you wish to supplement, simply add one crushed human multivitamin and 1 teaspoon of eggshell powder (page 193) to any meal recipe in this book.

🐾 If feeding more than 50 percent homemade meals, supplementation is highly recommended. Adding one crushed human multivitamin and 1 teaspoon of eggshell powder (page 193) to any meal recipe in this book will round out the nutrition within the same range as commercial foods.

🐾 Other supplements, such as fish oil, glucosamine, chondroitin, or MSM (methylsulfonylmethane), are also beneficial and can be used at your discretion and your veterinarian's recommendation.

A dog whose nose has been buried in a bowl of kibble for years may give you a funny look when you offer him a carrot. When you start sharing foods, following a few simple guidelines can prevent digestive upset and convince your dog that yes, a carrot is actually food.

Start with Teaspoons and Tablespoons, Not Cups and Handfuls

Every dog is different and some stomachs are more sensitive than others. Start out with a smaller amount per day to see how your dog tolerates different foods, especially if your pet has a history of digestive issues. And yes, you can write in the margin to take notes.

Exercise Moderation in Everything—Except Variety

There are a hundred foods you can feed your dog, each with its own unique benefits. Don't get stuck in a rut; the more variety your pet receives, the better it is for his overall health.

Try, Try Again

If you already provide fresh foods to your dog, you know her likes and dislikes and have a good idea of her preferences. When providing unfamiliar fresh foods to dogs, their reaction may range from hesitation to wild enthusiasm. Many of our dogs came to our household very suspicious of the foods I was offering them. I used a variety of techniques to get them accustomed to eating actual foods instead of just kibble:

🐾 Feeding something new first to a dog who is a good eater offers a positive role model.

🐾 Chopping new foods finely and mixing into other foods in the dog bowl helps dogs become accustomed to the foods.

🐾 If your dog can catch, toss the food in the air and see if she will eat it. Flying food often gets swallowed quicker.

🐾 Try using the Chicken Liver Cheat (page 44) or Bacon Powder (page 75) recipe as a meat-based "spice" to help entice your dog to try something new.

COOKIES AREN'T THE ONLY TREAT

A few cookie recipes are included in this book, but the real treats are simple foods right off your cutting board. The different foods represented here can all be a treat just by themselves or as ingredients in a variety of recipes. A cookie provides a crunchy treat for a moment, but real foods provide both a treat and unique nutrients to keep your dog healthy for a lifetime.

THIS INSTEAD OF THAT

Through my website and blog, I receive many questions on whether it's okay to make substitutions. My answer is almost always yes; however, I urge you not to replace so many ingredients that you're just using the same basic ingredients over and over. It's the variety of nutrition that makes a difference to your pet's overall health.

Cooking fats: I prefer to use coconut oil for the dogs and in much of my own meals. However, if you don't have coconut oil, by all means use olive or safflower oil. You'll also see in some cases that I'm not above using a little bacon fat to make a tail wag.

Fruits and vegetables: Substitute an equal amount of an ingredient for one that shares roughly the same amount of calories and similar nutrients:

- Potatoes, rutabagas, squashes, turnips, and yams

- Apples and carrots

- Broccoli and cauliflower

- Cantaloupe, mangoes, nectarines, papayas, peaches, pears, and plums

- Asparagus, bell peppers, green beans, peas, snow peas, and zucchini

- Collard greens, kale, lettuce, and spinach

Meats: The majority of the meals use a good amount of meats with slightly different calories for each classification. Substitute equal amounts of the following types of meats:

- Clams, mackerel, salmon, and sardines

- Lean beef stew meat, chicken breast or thighs, turkey breast or thighs

- 90% lean ground beef and country-style pork ribs

- 85% lean ground beef, lamb, and pork shoulder

Grains: Any grain can be substituted cup for cup calorie-wise, but they will offer slightly different amounts of protein. For more information on grains, see "Grains, Legumes & Seeds" (page 179). Cooking times and moisture may need to be adjusted to ensure grains are fully cooked and easy to digest. It's always better to add more water than not enough.

Herbs and spices can be substituted in equal amounts, but you can always add one or two of the spices mentioned throughout this book, for powerful antioxidant benefits.

HOW LARGE IS YOUR DOG'S BITE?

When preparing food for your dog, it's important to take into consideration the size of your dog's mouth when cutting meat and vegetables into manageable bite-size portions. Dogs do not chew each bite 30 times; instead, the majority of them gulp and swallow.

For the dogs under 40 pounds, I find it easier to just grind ingredients in a food processor rather than cutting into tiny dice. When cutting large quantities of meat by hand, freeze the meat for 30 minutes to firm it up and make slicing through it easier.

10- to 20-pound dogs: ¼ inch or ground

20- to 40-pound dogs: ½ inch or ground

40- to 60-pound dogs: ¾ inch

80- to 100-pound dogs: 1 inch

NO BEGGING AT THE TABLE

One of the most unfortunate reasons that people do not feed their dog real foods is they don't want their pet to beg at the table. I wholeheartedly agree that dogs should not be begging at the table, but it's the training, not the food, that is causing the problem. We practice a philosophy at home called "Always or Never." If dogs are fed from the table, in their mind there is *always a chance* they might get something. The occasional tidbit shared in the conditions you're trying to prevent reinforces the idea of opportunity in your dog. When you *never* feed your dog from the table, your pet learns begging doesn't pay off; he gets bored and learns a good nap feels better than watching somebody else eat.

At the same time, your dog so desperately wants a bite of something real, something delicious, rather than the same fare day after day. Maybe you are simultaneously thinking, "Couldn't I give my pup a little piece?" Sure, just not in the dining room.

The best place to provide your dog with real food is in her bowl. It doesn't have to be a meal; it can just be a quick chop or a fast sauté of some ingredients you are making for yourself. I would still recommend doing this after you've finished eating rather than before, to reward good behavior.

At my home, when we're eating in the dining room, the dogs are not allowed to enter. Instead, those who behaved get a treat delivered to them in the living room; we don't call the dogs into the dining room when we're done because having them come to us would reinforce the idea we're all dining together.

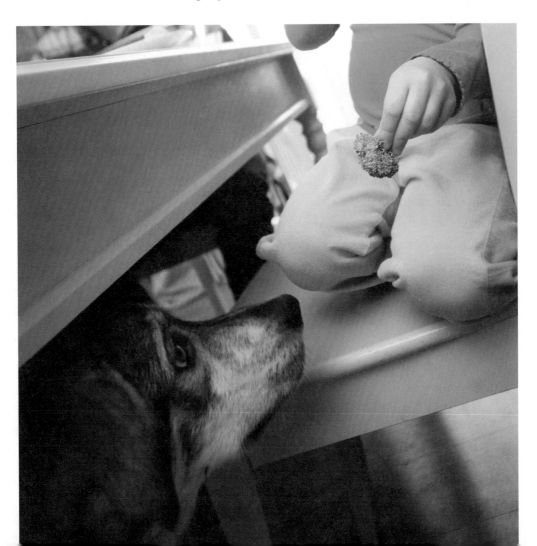

Another option is to feed your dog with a Kong for distraction while you're eating. My dogs and I are big fans of the Kong and I stuff them like a puzzle to be solved, to earn 20 minutes of peace and quiet.

I do fail in one way, and I pay the price. I'm klutzy. When I'm cooking, I occasionally drop something on the floor and the dogs race to get the prize. Through hundreds of "oops" accidents I've trained our dogs to be vigilant while I'm cooking. I have to shoo them out of the kitchen five or six times a night while they're on patrol for my carelessness. I'm more cautious now; when I drop something, I pick it up and take it to the dog that remains seated outside the kitchen.

THE BEST KITCHEN ACCESSORY IS A HUNGRY DOG

Sharing foods with your dog doesn't require any special equipment other than a good dog bowl. However, cooking for yourself and/or for your pet becomes much easier when you have the right equipment. Here are some of my favorite tools:

- *Good sharp knives and a cleaver*: Having your knives sharpened by a professional makes all the difference. Suddenly you're able to slice tomatoes with ease. Seek out knife sharpeners at farmers' markets or at your local grocery store (ask the butcher!). When your knives are super sharp, you'll need a break-in period to become accustomed to how well your knives work; take it slow the first few times out of the knife block. A good heavy cleaver is also a blessing when dealing with squashes, yams, and whole chickens.

- *Food processor*: When it comes to grating or chopping, dogs don't care whether you use an electric appliance to get the job done. A good food processor can cut your chopping or grating time to 10 percent of what it would take by hand. When cooking for dogs that weigh fewer than 20 pounds, consider grinding meat with a food processor instead of cutting it into bite-size bits.

❧ *Silicone baking sheet liners*: I rarely used our silicone liners until recently, and now I send everything through the oven with one lining the baking pan. Cleanup is a snap, there's less need for additional cooking oils, and the food still browns well.

❧ *Microplane grater*: With different sizes of grating options, this is one of my favorite tools for grating Parmesan cheese, ginger, fresh turmeric, or even small amounts of vegetables.

❧ *Poultry shears*: A good set of curvy poultry shears makes short work of jobs that usually call for knives.

❧ *Pizza cutter*: I try to be practical when making dog treats; cutting them into bone shapes seems pointless when the dogs aren't going to notice. I usually just cut cookies into one-inch squares using a pizza cutter just before I pop them in the oven. When I want to get fancy, I use a ravioli cutter with a fluted edge and cut on a diagonal. I'm more concerned with what goes into the cookie than with the shape. The dogs are, too.

❧ *Separate freezer*: An extra freezer is worth the investment. I buy items on sale and freeze them, and I'm known to squirrel away extra vegetables for use in dog food. My freezer has probably paid for itself in the last few years just based upon what I've saved in buying chicken stock; at any given time there are three or four chicken carcasses in the freezer waiting to be turned into stock and a few quarts of homemade stock already prepared.

CHAPTER 1

MEAT MAKES THE MEAL

If you're going to make a meal for your dog, it ought to be based on meat. (Dogs in particular are the most ardent supporters of this philosophy.) Not only is meat the driving force of your dog's appetite, it's also what's going to provide what your pet needs most: protein.

While there is solid information on the recommended daily allowance (RDA) of protein and the minimums required to support functions in a dog's body, there is a vast gray area when it comes to how much is too much. Even if there were a precise target for all dogs, it might not be right for your dog. Every breed, every age, every dog is a little different. The meals throughout this book are based upon 50 percent of your dog's calories coming from meat. Conveniently, this equals about a pound of meat and fulfills your dog's protein requirement by 200 to 300 percent and the fat requirement by 100 to 400 percent, depending on the recipe and meat used.

If you have difficulty finding various cuts of meats used in this book, ask the butcher at your grocery store. If the butcher doesn't have it, the store may be able to order it for you. Another great resource is localharvest.org, where you can find farmers in your area who can sell to you directly.

OTHER INGREDIENTS

Beyond meat, most people are going to need to supplement their dog's diet with some form of carbohydrate. Carbohydrates found in fruits, vegetables, grains, or legumes provide the body with easily accessible energy, fiber to help digestion, and unique combinations of vitamins, minerals, and antioxidants. We have four classes of carbohydrates to choose from, each with benefits as well as calls for moderation:

- *Non-starchy vegetables and fruits*: Green leafy vegetables, broccoli, tomatoes, berries, and so on are lower in calories and all contain beneficial phytochemicals that should be part of your dog's diet. However, some of these ingredients can be high in oxalates or too acidic and so should be included in the diet in moderate amounts.

- *Starchy vegetables and fruits*: Potatoes, yams, turnips, rutabagas, bananas, and so on are also fairly low in calories, high in fiber, and bring along many antioxidants to build a stronger pup. Many of these items range from medium to high on the glycemic index (which means they raise blood sugar levels); this is balanced by including an appropriate amount of protein and fat in the recipes.

- *Legumes*: Various beans, peas, and lentils bring in another healthy dose of protein to complement meat-based meals along with fiber and carbohydrates for energy. Again, we're looking for moderation because nobody likes a gassy dog.

- *Grains*: Quinoa, millet, rice, buckwheat, and oats are concentrated sources of calories (around 600 calories per cup of uncooked grain), providing protein in addition to carbohydrates and fiber. Because grains are more difficult for dogs to digest, they often need to be prepared with more water or stock to make them softer and easier to digest. Adding 2 to 3 cups of cooking liquid per cup of grain brings down the calories per cup to about half of that of commercial dry foods, filling up your dog with fewer calories. However, grains aren't perfect—they can be high glycemic, which causes blood sugar to spike; they may cause gluten sensitivities to react; or they can be used in excess (or even worse, as the primary source of protein) in a dog's diet. I've chosen a moderate amount of grains for those recipes that call for them.

Each dog is different and each pet owner's reasoning is different. I've included meals based primarily upon meat as well as with each of these types of carbohydrates. My goal is to give you options with ingredients in reasonable quantities and facts to help you make your choice. Whether you include different carbohydrates because it works for your dog or your budget, or you are selecting ingredients familiar to you and you can readily share, that's your personal choice and you'll find plenty of recipes to meet your needs.

ABOUT THE RECIPES

Most of the meal recipes can also be made in a slow cooker, simply by combining the ingredients and allowing them to simmer on the LOW setting for 6 to 8 hours. I supersize the recipes for the slow cooker by tripling the ingredients. This also happens to be the right amount for using ⅓ cup of the Supplement Stew recipe in my book *Feed Your Best Friend Better*.

All meals can be refrigerated for up to 4 days or frozen for up to 1 month.

Each recipe is accompanied with information on how the key nutrients (calories, protein, fats, and carbohydrates) are met. Complete nutritional information for every recipe, with and without supplementation, is available for free at dogfooddude.com.

EGGS

When you crack open an egg, the contents seem pretty simple: a watery-looking white surrounding a yellow-orange yolk. Don't let the illusion of simplicity fool you; the egg is actually a powerhouse of nutrition.

The purpose of the white is to protect and nourish the yolk so it can develop into a baby chick. Inside your dog's body, the nutrients in the white carry out the same function, but will focus on growing fur, not feathers. The white provides the bulk of the proteins to build strong muscles, enabling your dog to jump onto the forbidden couch when you aren't home. While your pet is snoozing on the couch, all the essential proteins he needs will be repairing muscle tissue, creating collagen, building bone, and protecting the heart.

Shrouded inside the yolk are the fat-soluble vitamins A, B (folate), D, E, and K, and the antioxidants lutein and zeaxanthin, which keep your dog's eyes healthy. When your dog sees your car pull up into the driveway, he knows to jump off the couch because the omega-3 fatty acid DHA has built a solid structure in the brain, while amino acids and choline have created neurotransmitters that play an important role in learning and memory.

The color of the eggs does not matter as much how the hen they came from was fed. Organic, free-range eggs from hens eating grass and other vegetation, not just chicken feed, will be more nutritious. Duck eggs, if you can find them, are even higher in omega-3 fatty acids and choline; look for these if your dog needs an extra memory boost in learning to stay off that couch.

When baking, you often need just an egg white or just the yolks. Make the extra parts into a quick omelet for your dog, using another egg to even things out a bit. Both the white and yolk are healthy additions to your dog's diet and adding another egg ensures your pet receives the benefits from both parts of the egg.

SCRAMBLE FOR BREAKFAST

There are two mistakes people make when feeding their dogs eggs: They don't feed them often enough or they feel they need to make a fresh scrambled egg every morning. You can solve both issues by cooking three to four days' worth of eggs at one time.

INGREDIENTS
4 to 8 large eggs

1. Start your morning coffee.

2. Heat a nonstick skillet over medium heat.

3. Beat the eggs in a small bowl, using a fork or whisk.

4. Pour the eggs into the pan and allow them to cook for 3 minutes. With a spatula, lift up one-quarter of the eggs and turn them over, then repeat with remaining portions.

5. Cook the eggs for 2 more minutes, until they are set and dry.

6. Your coffee should just be finishing, so help yourself to a cup while your dog's eggs are cooling to room temperature.

7. Extra portions can be refrigerated in an airtight container for up to 3 days.

KEY NUTRIENTS

Calories 9% • Protein 26% • Total fats 36% • Carbohydrates 0.72 g • Sodium 37% • Selenium 18% • A 22% • B_5 (pantothenic acid) 21% • B_6 (pyridoxine) 23% • B_9 (folate) 36% • Choline 30% • D 31%

1 large egg has about 71 calories; equivalent to about ⅕ cup of commercial dry food.

Replace 10% of your dog's regular meal with the below amounts:

10-lb. dog
½ large egg

20-lb. dog
⅔ large egg

40-lb. dog
1 large egg

60-lb. dog
1½ large egg

80-lb. dog
2 large eggs

100-lb. dog
2½ large eggs

FRITTATA

Because eggs are a moderately inflammatory food, I often combine them with anti-inflammatory kale and butternut squash, especially for senior dogs. This meal ends up being very low in calories and a great source of protein, fiber, and antioxidants.

Try making this for your dog, then try making another for yourself. It's simple and, with a little salt and pepper and a topping of Parmesan cheese, it'll be a welcome addition to your breakfast or dinner table.

INGREDIENTS

1 tablespoon coconut or olive oil
3 cups diced or grated (use a food processor) butternut squash
½ cup chopped kale
6 large eggs

1. Heat the oil in a heavy skillet over medium-high heat. (Do not use a nonstick pan, because higher than medium heat can break down the pan's coating.)

2. Add the squash and cook for 15 minutes, stirring occasionally. The squash should be lightly browned at the edges and very tender.

3. Sprinkle the kale over the squash.

4. Whisk the eggs and add to the skillet. Cook for 5 minutes.

5. Remove from the heat and cover with a lid. Let the frittata rest for 10 minutes, or until the eggs have completely firmed up.

6. Allow the frittata to cool, then cut into portions for your dog. Store any extra in the refrigerator for up to 3 days.

Yield: 3⅓ cups

KEY NUTRIENTS

231 calories per cup • Protein 202% • Carbohydrate-to-protein ratio 1.3 to 1 • Total fats 355%

Serve the following amount as a meal, twice a day:

10-lb. dog
½ to ¾ cup

20-lb. dog
1 to 1⅓ cups

40-lb. dog
1⅔ to 2⅓ cups

60-lb. dog
2 to 3 cups

80-lb. dog
2½ to 3¾ cups

100-lb. dog
3 to 4½ cups

GROUND BEEF

The amount of fat included in the making of a hamburger can make a big difference in the nutrition your dog is getting out of a simple patty.

Quarter Pounder for an 80-Pounder

Here's the nutrients ¼ pound of ground beef will provide to an 80-pound dog:

> 70% lean/30% fat ground beef:
> Calories: 24%
> Protein: 34%
> Fat: 128%

> 85% lean/15% fat ground beef:
> Calories: 15%
> Protein: 44%
> Fat: 64%

> 90% lean/10% fat ground beef:
> Calories: 12%
> Protein: 47%
> Fat: 43%

My recommendations for choosing ground beef based upon the usage are:

🐾 *To supplement commercial dry foods*: Ninety percent lean will help even out the fat in commercial food and supply a good amount of quality protein.

🐾 *Primarily in meat-based homemade foods*: When feeding a dog a primarily meat-based diet, I would still advise using the 90% lean because even if this is only half of your dog's diet, it will be almost 200 percent of the fat and protein needed per day. I recommend some type of starchy vegetables, such as 1¼ pounds of yam per pound of meat, to help normalize the protein and fat content.

♣ *Homemade foods containing greater than 1 cup of grain per pound of meat*: The 85% lean fat mixture provides a nice ratio when combined with starches, such as oats or rice. Two cups of oats (plus 2 cups of water) or 1 cup of brown rice (cooked in 3 cups of water) helps bring your dog's meal to about 215 percent of the fat RDA and 240 percent of the protein RDA.

Does buying organic or grass-fed matter? You bet! Meat from grass-fed animals contains 500 percent of the conjugated linoleic acid (CLA) found in industrial-fed meat. CLA has been shown to reduce fat and fight various stages of cancer. Whenever possible, look for grass-fed meat for both you and your pups.

JUST THE BURGER, HOLD THE BUN

When you're fixing burgers for yourself, it's simple to make an extra patty for your best friend. There's no need to get fancy with a bun, tomatoes, lettuce, pickles, and cheese. (Your dog may not agree with me on the cheese.) What your pet really wants is the beef, and with this recipe, he only needs to wait 10 minutes.

INGREDIENTS

½ pound 90% lean ground beef
1 clove garlic, minced
½ teaspoon fresh rosemary, or ¼ teaspoon dried (optional, but should be
    omitted for dogs prone to seizures)

1. Heat a nonstick skillet over medium heat.

2. Crumble the beef into the skillet. Sprinkle the garlic and rosemary over the beef and cook for 10 minutes, stirring occasionally.

Yield: 1 cup

KEY NUTRIENTS

Calories 17% • Protein 63% • Total fats 57% • Potassium 24% • Iron 23% • Zinc 25% • B$_3$ (niacin) 92% • B$_6$ (pyridoxine) 77%

1 cup of beef stew meat has 290 calories; equivalent to about ¾ cup of commercial dry food.

Replace one-third of your dog's normal meal with the following amounts:

10-lb. dog
3 tablespoons

20-lb. dog
¼ cup

40-lb. dog
⅓ cup

60-lb. dog
½ cup

80-lb. dog
⅔ cup

100-lb. dog
¾ cup

BUTTERED UP WITH BEEF

This meal easily satisfies all of your dog's protein requirements and provides vitamin A to keep your pet's eyes healthy and fiber to keep her full. Chopping the butternut squash in a food processor makes this much easier. If you're cutting the squash by hand, cut into ½-inch dice.

INGREDIENTS

2 cups water
4½ cups chopped butternut squash (1½ pounds)
1 pound 90% lean ground beef
1 cup spinach

1. Combine the water and butternut squash in a large, heavy skillet over high heat.

2. Bring to a simmer, then lower the heat to medium.

3. Cook, uncovered, for 10 minutes, or until most of the water has evaporated and the squash has softened slightly.

4. Stir in the beef and spinach and cook over medium heat for 20 minutes.

Yield: 6 cups

KEY NUTRIENTS

192 calories per cup • Protein 311% • Carbohydrate-to-protein ratio 0.8 to 1 • Total fats 258%

Serve the following amount as a meal, twice a day:

10-lb. dog
⅔ to 1 cup

20-lb. dog
1 to 1⅔ cups

40-lb. dog
2 to 2¾ cups

60-lb. dog
2⅓ to 3¾ cups

80-lb. dog
3 to 4⅔ cups

100-lb. dog
3½ to 5½ cups

GINGERED BEEF & BROCCOLI

A quick stir-fry of meat and vegetables is an easy way to make dinner for yourself. Just as easy is a grain-free preparation for your pet that's low in carbohydrates and full of flavor and healthy vegetables. This is a great meal by itself or it can be used to replace an equal amount of your dog's regular meal.

INGREDIENTS

1 teaspoon grated fresh ginger
1 red bell pepper, seeded and diced
½ cup chopped broccoli
1 cup finely chopped cabbage
1½ pounds 90% lean ground beef
¼ cup water (optional)

1. Mix the ginger and vegetables together in a large, nonstick skillet and crumble the beef over the top.

2. Cook over medium heat for 20 minutes, stirring occasionally.

3. The vegetables should be very tender; if they need a few more minutes, add ¼ cup of water and let them simmer gently for another 5 minutes.

Yield: 5 cups

KEY NUTRIENTS

254 calories per cup • Protein 381% • Carbohydrate-to-protein ratio 0.1 to 1 •
Total fats 342%

Serve the following amount as a meal, twice a day:

10-lb. dog
½ to ¾ cup

20-lb. dog
¾ to 1¼ cups

40-lb. dog
1½ to 2 cups

60-lb. dog
1¾ to 2¾ cups

80-lb. dog
2¼ to 3½ cups

100-lb. dog
2¾ to 4 cups

GROUND AND BROWNED

Since you're combining beef with rice in this recipe, you can use beef with a little more fat. With all the beefy flavor, your dog won't even notice we snuck in some kale.

INGREDIENTS

2 cups water
1 cup chopped carrot
½ cup uncooked brown rice
¾ pound 85% lean ground beef
½ cup chopped kale

1. Bring the water to a boil in a 2-quart saucepan over high heat and then stir in the carrot, rice, and beef.

2. Allow the water to return to a boil before lowering the heat to low.

3. Cover the pot and simmer for 45 minutes.

4. Stir in the kale, re-cover the pot, and simmer for 15 minutes, or until all the liquid is absorbed.

Yield: 4 cups

KEY NUTRIENTS

229 calories per cup • Protein 221% • Carbohydrate-to-protein ratio 1.2 to 1 • Total fats 299% • Antioxidants 40%

Serve the following amount as a meal, twice a day:

10-lb. dog
½ to ¾ cup

20-lb. dog
1 to 1⅓ cups

40-lb. dog
1⅔ to 2⅓ cups

60-lb. dog
2 to 3 cups

80-lb. dog
2½ to 4 cups

100-lb. dog
3 to 4⅔ cups

BEEF THAT GOES BY THE NAME CHUCK

The traditional Sunday night dinner may not happen as much as I would like these days. However, when friends and family gather, it's a time to celebrate, and more often than not our friends bring their dogs. While one of us runs around frantically cleaning the house and picking up the 30 or so dog toys strewn about, the other person is in the kitchen making a meal from scratch, which often includes a roast. We aim to feed *all* of our family and friends well, even the guests walking around on four paws. So, when we go to the butcher, we ask for a slightly larger cut of meat, usually a quarter to half of a pound. We get a little enthusiastic with spices and different treatments for our roast and we don't want to send anybody's dog home with an upset stomach, so we just trim an extra portion off the roast before we prep it. When it's time to say good night, I know all of our guests are happy when the pups run back into the kitchen for one final check of the food bowls.

Any of the following meals can use an equal amount of 90% or leaner ground beef in place of the beef chuck.

4- OR 15-MINUTE STEAK BITES

If you just want to trim a little bit of the roast and give it a quick cooking, there are two methods, based on how much time you want to spend at the stove. They're both quick, but depending on how busy I am, I use different pans. A nonstick pan will break down if heated higher than medium temperature, so I use that for the slower-cooking version, and cast iron for a quick fry.

4-Minute Steak Bites

INGREDIENTS

½ pound beef roast or stew meat (1 cup)
1 garlic clove, minced (optional)
¼ cup water

1. Heat a stainless-steel or cast-iron skillet over medium-high heat.

2. While the skillet is heating, cut the beef into bite-size cubes (see page xv).

3. Place the beef and garlic (if using) in the skillet and allow them to cook for about 1 minute. When the meat starts to release easily, stir around the pan for the remaining 2 minutes.

4. Add the water and turn off the heat. The water will help deglaze the pan, while making a little sauce and making cleanup easier. Stir the beef and rub at the sides of the pan to release any brown bits for about a minute.

Yield: 1 cup

1 cup of beef stew meat has 290 calories; equivalent to about ¾ cup of commercial dry food.

Replace one-third of your dog's normal meal with the following amounts:

10-lb. dog
¼ cup

20-lb. dog
⅓ cup

40-lb. dog
⅔ cup

60-lb. dog
¾ cup

80-lb. dog
1 cup

100-lb. dog
1¼ cups

15-Minute Steak Bites

INGREDIENTS
½ pound beef roast or stew meat
1 garlic clove, minced (optional)

1. Cut the beef into bite-size cubes (see page xv).

2. Heat a nonstick skillet over medium heat.

3. Place the beef and garlic (if using) in the skillet and allow them to cook for 4 to 5 minutes, until lightly browned. Stir every 3 to 4 minutes to brown on all sides.

Yield: 1 cup

KEY NUTRIENTS

Calories 18% • Protein 102% • Total fats 38% • Phosphorus 33% • Potassium 40% • Iron 33% • Selenium 31% • Zinc 42% • B_3 (niacin) 135% • B_6 (pyridoxine) 178% • B_{12} (cyanocobalamin) 31%

BEEF & 3 C'S CASSEROLE

As you read through the section on vegetables and how they are important for both you and your dog, you'll find yourself packing the produce bin a little fuller. Here's a way to share some of those same vegetables with your dog.

For a dog requiring a lot of energy but needing to stay clear of carbohydrates, this hearty casserole is higher in fat with a good amount of protein and fiber to balance things out. Layering the beef on top of the vegetables allows the veggies to soak up the delicious beef flavor.

INGREDIENTS

1 pound beef chuck roast
2 cups chopped cauliflower
1 cup chopped chard
1 cup chopped carrot
½ cup water

1. Preheat the oven to 400°F.

2. While the oven heats, cube the beef into bite-size cubes (see page xv).

3. In an 8-inch square casserole, layer in the cauliflower, chard, and carrot, then top with the beef.

4. Cover with a lid or foil and bake for 45 minutes.

Yield: 5 cups

KEY NUTRIENTS

252 calories per cup • Protein 228% • Carbohydrate-to-protein ratio 0.3 to 1 • Total fats 462% • Antioxidants 84%

Serve the following amount as a meal, twice a day:

10-lb. dog
½ to ¾ cup

20-lb. dog
¾ to 1¼ cups

40-lb. dog
1½ to 2 cups

60-lb. dog
1¾ to 2¾ cups

80-lb. dog
2⅓ to 3½ cups

100-lb. dog
2¾ to 4¼ cups

BEEF, QUINOA, & GREEN BEANS

Quinoa is one of the quickest grains to cook, is easily digested, and contains a higher carbohydrate-to-protein ratio than any other grain. It's appearing more often in restaurants and on dinner plates at home. Here's a simple recipe pairing quinoa with beef and green beans for your dog, who will appreciate the protein and how easy it is to digest.

INGREDIENTS

3½ cups water
1 cup uncooked quinoa
½ pound beef chuck roast, cut into bite-size chunks (see page xv)
1 cup chopped fresh or frozen green beans

1. Bring the water to a boil in a 2-quart saucepan over high heat.

2. Add the quinoa, beef, and green beans, cover the pan, and lower the heat to low.

3. Cook for 40 minutes, or until the quinoa has absorbed all the water.

Yield: 4½ cups

KEY NUTRIENTS

278 calories per cup • Protein 180% • Carbohydrate-to-protein ratio 1.8 to 1 •
Total fats 284% • Antioxidants 100%

Serve the following amount
as a meal, twice a day:

10-lb. dog
⅓ to ¾ cup

20-lb. dog
¾ to 1 cup

40-lb. dog
1⅓ to 2 cups

60-lb. dog
1¾ to 2⅔ cups

80-lb. dog
2 to 3¼ cups

100-lb. dog
2⅓ to 3¾ cups

STOLEN ROAST

Stories of dogs' absconding with a roast intended for the family dinner can be both funny and aggravating. Let your dog know there is no reason to turn to a life a crime, by stealing an inch of your roast and some snow peas from your salad. Toss them with a couple of other ingredients and cook alongside your own dinner, so everybody gets a warm meal and nobody has to spend time in the doghouse.

INGREDIENTS

1 tablespoon coconut or olive oil
4½ cups seeded and cubed butternut squash (1½ pounds)
1 cup snow peas, chopped
1 large apple, cored and diced
⅔ pound beef chuck roast, cut into bite-size chunks (about 1⅓ cups; see page xv)
1 teaspoon nutritional yeast

1. Preheat the oven to 350°F. Grease an 8-inch square baking dish with the oil.

2. Combine the butternut squash, snow peas, and apple in the dish.

3. Layer the beef on top of the mixture and cover with foil.

4. Bake for 1 hour.

Yield: 6¼ cups

KEY NUTRIENTS

198 calories per cup • Protein 176% • Carbohydrate-to-protein ratio 1.9 to 1 •
Total fats 314% • Antioxidants 297%

Serve the following amount as a meal, twice a day:

10-lb. dog
⅔ to 1 cup

20-lb. dog
1 to 1⅔ cups

40-lb. dog
2 to 2¾ cups

60-lb. dog
2⅓ to 3⅔ cups

80-lb. dog
3 to 4½ cups

100-lb. dog
3⅓ to 5⅓ cups

CHUNKS OF CHUCK, RICE, & VEGGIES

At the dinner table, people eat a lot of dishes served over rice because rice soaks up the flavor and sauces. For your dog, we're going to put the flavor right into the rice by simmering the rice with the same ingredients you can use in a stir-fry.

INGREDIENTS

2 cups homemade stock (beef or chicken can be used, provided your dog has no sensitivities)

1 cup water

½ pound beef stew meat (or 90% lean ground beef), chopped into bite-size pieces (see page xv)

1 cup uncooked brown rice

1 cup chopped green beans

½ cup chopped carrot

¼ cup seeded and chopped red bell pepper

1. Bring the stock and water to a boil in a 2-quart saucepan over high heat.

2. Add the remaining ingredients and stir to combine.

3. Cover tightly and lower the heat to a simmer.

4. Simmer for 1 hour, or until all the liquid has been absorbed.

Yield: 6 cups

KEY NUTRIENTS

206 calories per cup • Protein 221% • Carbohydrate-to-protein ratio 2.3 to 1 • Total fats 110% • Antioxidants 125%

Serve the following amount as a meal, twice a day:

10-lb. dog
⅔ to 1 cup

20-lb. dog
1 to 1½ cups

40-lb. dog
1¾ to 2½ cups

60-lb. dog
2¼ to 3½ cups

80-lb. dog
2¾ to 4⅓ cups

100-lb. dog
3⅓ to 5 cups

NOT TOO CHILI FOR KALE

The simplest chilis are often the best, and even better when simmered for hours. Many of the same ingredients in your own chili are cooked here in a fraction of the time. If your dog isn't a huge vegetable lover, try this meat-based chili with a few healthy vegetables thrown in. It's pretty likely he will lick the bowl clean, kale and all.

INGREDIENTS

2 pounds beef stew meat (or lean chuck), chopped into bite-size pieces (see page xv)
1 clove garlic, minced
½ teaspoon ground cumin
¼ teaspoon ground cinnamon
¾ cup seeded and chopped red bell pepper
½ cup chopped tomatoes
1 cup chopped kale

1. Heat a large skillet over medium heat.

2. Place the meat, garlic, and cumin in the pan and stir to combine. Brown the meat on all sides by giving it a stir every 5 minutes for a total 25 minutes.

3. Stir the peppers, tomatoes, and kale into the browned meat.

4. Cover and cook for 10 minutes longer.

Yield: 4½ cups

KEY NUTRIENTS

279 calories per cup • Protein 560% • Carbohydrate-to-protein ratio 0.1 to 1 • Total fats 212% • Antioxidants 133%

Serve the following amount as a meal, twice a day:

10-lb. dog
⅓ to ¾ cup

20-lb. dog
¾ to 1 cup

40-lb. dog
1⅓ to 2 cups

60-lb. dog
1⅔ to 2⅔ cups

80-lb. dog
2 to 3¼ cups

100-lb. dog
2⅓ to 3¾ cups

SIMPLY BEEF & YAM

You have a decision to make with this dish: Do you take your dog out for a walk while it's roasting or do you tempt your pet indoors with the delicious aromas of a new favorite meal while it's cooking? Our dog Flynn loves walks, but he's just as likely to sit and wait in front of the oven when this beefy meal is cooking.

INGREDIENTS

1 tablespoon coconut or olive oil
1 pound beef stew meat or lean chuck, chopped into bite-size pieces or
   ground (see page xv)
3 cups cubed Garnet yam
¼ cup chopped fresh parsley
1 teaspoon dried oregano, or 1 tablespoon fresh (omit for dogs that are
   prone to seizures)

1. Preheat the oven to 350°F. Grease an 8-inch square baking
   dish with the oil.

2. Combine all the remaining ingredients in the baking dish and
   toss well.

3. Bake for 50 minutes.

Yield: 4¾ cups

KEY NUTRIENTS

260 calories per cup • Protein 297% •
Carbohydrate-to-protein ratio 1.2 to 1 •
Total fats 178%

Serve the following amount
as a meal, twice a day:

10-lb. dog
½ to ¾ cup

20-lb. dog
¾ to 1¼ cups

40-lb. dog
1⅓ to 2 cups

60-lb. dog
1¾ to 2⅔ cups

80-lb. dog
2¼ to 3⅓ cups

100-lb. dog
2⅔ to 4 cups

BEEF TRAINING TREATS

When I find a good deal on lean beef, this is the treat I make for the dogs. Overall it can be less expensive than high-quality store-bought treats and you have total control over what goes into the treats. Plus you get a light stock that goes great over your dog's meal. I've seen many recipes for similar treats that take hours at low heat to dry. The secret to these is to boil them first, which helps dry the treats faster.

INGREDIENTS

2 pounds lean beef (stew meat works great)
3 cups water
1 teaspoon garlic powder (optional)
1 teaspoon coconut or olive oil

1. Preheat the oven to 375°F.

2. Cut the meat into ½-inch cubes. I use poultry shears because they snip away at slippery meat faster than using a knife.

3. Bring the water to a boil in a 2-quart saucepan.

4. Add the beef and allow the water to return to a boil before lowering the heat to medium-low.

5. Simmer for 10 minutes, covered.

6. Drain the stock and reserve for other use.

7. Toss the beef, garlic powder, and oil on a rimmed baking sheet until the meat is lightly coated.

8. Bake for 45 minutes, or until dry and crispy.

Yield: 200 treats

KEY NUTRIENTS

6 calories per treat or 11% of your dog's daily calories • Protein 57% • Carbohydrate-to-protein ratio 0 to 1 • Total fats 24%

Daily allowance:

10-lb. dog
5 treats

20-lb. dog
10 treats

40-lb. dog
15 treats

60-lb. dog
20 treats

80-lb. dog
30 treats

100-lb. dog
35 treats

CHICKEN BONES & BROTH

Your dog always knew there was something delicious and full of nutrition inside bones; here's your chance to confirm it. As the bones cook down, they release calcium, phosphorus, magnesium, potassium, and proteins found inside the bone. In addition, the chondroitin and glucosamine is extracted from the cartilage. Where does it all go? It stays in the broth. The difference between the chicken stock you buy in a store and homemade bone broth is quite apparent when you make it. Bone broth isn't the same weak yellow color as chicken stock; it's richly colored, opaque, and as it cools the gelatin from the bones firms it up. It seems that even people are catching on to what dogs already know, with recipes for bone broth appearing more often—even restaurants that specialize in bone broth are opening.

The finished broth is great all on its own, used to cook vegetables and grains, or just pouring over your dog's food to make it extra tempting. When dogs aren't eating much, they will often at least take some sips of bone broth to help hydrate them and prepare them for coming back to full appetite mode. Plus, bone broth has healing properties for the stomach.

Adding apple cider vinegar to the broth helps break down the bones. Remember the science experiment in grade school where you covered a chicken bone in vinegar and left it for a few days? The reason the bone became flexible is that vinegar helps extract the calcium, leaving behind just soft, flexible bone tissue.

BENEFICIAL BONE BROTH

If you have extra vegetables in the fridge that are safe for dogs, go ahead and throw in a couple of cups. I've added everything from apples to lettuce and, of course, the traditional carrots. If your dog has a favorite fruit or vegetable, get creative!

INGREDIENTS

1 pound chicken bones
1 tablespoon apple cider vinegar
6 cups water

1. Combine all the ingredients in a slow cooker and cook on LOW for 24 hours. That's right, 24! Start it before you go to bed and it will be ready to strain just after dinner the next day.

2. Strain the broth, using a fine-mesh strainer. When making bone broth for our meals, I discard the solids right away. When I make it for the dogs, I press on the bones with a wooden spoon until they start to disintegrate, then mash the bones around a bit in the strainer to press out the extra calcium and marrow inside; finally, I discard the remaining solids.

3. Store the bone broth in the refrigerator for up to 4 days or in the freezer for up to 3 months.

Yield: 5 cups

KEY NUTRIENTS

200 calories per cup • Protein 13% • Carbohydrate-to-protein ratio 1.1 to 1 • Total fats 37% • Antioxidants 238%

Replace 10% of your dog's meal with the following amounts:

10-lb. dog
3 tablespoons

20-lb. dog
⅓ cup

40-lb. dog
½ cup

60-lb. dog
⅔ cup

80-lb. dog
¾ cup

100-lb. dog
1 cup

CHICKEN STOCK GRANITA

To make this granita, the vegetables are processed with some of the liquid, so the end product is very smooth. If your bone broth is really rich, you can always use half broth and half water.

INGREDIENTS
4 cups homemade stock or bone broth (page 25), divided
1 cup finely chopped vegetables.

1. Chill a large, rimmed baking sheet in the freezer for 1 hour, arranging the sheet so it is lying completely flat with enough headroom for you to hold a mug just above it.

2. Place 1 cup of the stock and all the vegetables in a food processor or blender and process until the vegetables have been reduced to a fine texture.

3. Stir the rest of the stock into the vegetables.

4. Without removing the baking sheet from the freezer, use a coffee mug or liquid measuring cup to ladle the mixture into the baking sheet. (Trust me, don't try carrying the full sheet to the freezer.)

5. Chill for 30 minutes and then rake with a fork in each direction.

6. Chill for another 30 minutes and then rake again in each direction. At this point it should be nice and slushy. You can scoop it into a bowl now or freeze for another 20 minutes, if needed.

Yield: about 5 cups

Follow the serving sizes for the bone broth (page 25).

STOCK SORBET

I'm always trying to find new ideas to cool down the dogs, and this was the first recipe I made with my new ice cream machine.

INGREDIENTS

4 cups homemade stock or bone broth (page 25)
1 cup finely chopped vegetables

1. Chill the ice cream tub according to your manufacturer's directions.

2. Place the stock and vegetables in the chilled tub, attach the mixing blade and top, then turn on the machine. In 20 minutes you'll have a money-saving, cool-down treat for your dog.

Yield: about 5 cups

Follow the serving sizes for the bone broth (page 25).

JUST BROTH—NOW IT'S GRAVY

Stock is nice, bone broth is better, but gravy is the best. This gravy is simple and provides something to stick to whatever else is in the dog bowl, making everything taste delicious. Ask your pet and see which she likes best. Once chilled, the gravy becomes solid, making this a good Kong stuffing as well.

INGREDIENTS

2 cups homemade bone broth (page 25)
2 tablespoons cornstarch or tapioca flour

1. Combine the bone broth and cornstarch in a 2-quart saucepan.

2. Bring to a boil over medium-high heat and then lower the heat to low. Whisk every few minutes until thick, 8 to 10 minutes.

Yield: 1½ cups

Follow the serving sizes for the bone broth (page 25).

CHICKEN BREAST AND CHICKEN TENDERS

With the advance of age, senior dogs are often less active and thus often a little thicker in the waistline. When your dog still retains a healthy appetite but needs some loving in the form of calorie counting, chicken breast is a good choice. The following portion sizes provide only 11 percent of your pet's recommended daily fat intake to moderate the average fat found in commercial dry foods, which hovers around 215 percent for senior formulas and 273 percent for other formulations. With the fat content being so low, you are left with some room for using healthier fats in the cooking process (read more about coconut oil on page 190) without sacrificing the goal of losing a little weight.

Vitamins B_3 (niacin) and B_6 (pyridoxine) and the amino acid glycine are all well represented in chicken breast. These nutrients help move stored energy into the cells of the body. When your dog's cells are charged up, it's more likely your pet will be as well.

Chicken tenders are the breast meat closest to the rib cage. They're almost identical to the nutrition in chicken breasts, with a little more protein and a little less fat, and often a 20 percent cost savings over boneless, skinless chicken breasts.

BREAST FOR BEASTS

This is a quick sauté you can do while you're chopping vegetables for your own dinner. Throw some of those same vegetables in the pan and you're adding both filling fiber and extra vitamins. It's much easier to cut the meat after you're done cooking.

INGREDIENTS

1 pound chicken breast
¼ teaspoon ground cumin

1. Spread a single layer of chicken in a nonstick skillet over medium heat and sprinkle with the cumin.

2. Cook for 10 minutes, then turn over and cook for 10 more minutes, so the chicken is cooked through.

3. Allow the chicken to cool, then cut into bite-size chunks for your dog (see page xv).

Yield: 2 cups

KEY NUTRIENTS

Calories 17% • Protein 105% • Total fats 22% • Phosphorus 33% • Magnesium 22% • Potassium 37% • Selenium 30% • B$_3$ (niacin) 259% • B$_6$ (pyridoxine) 254%

1 cup of beef stew meat has 290 calories; equivalent to about ¾ cup of commercial dry food.

Replace one-third of your dog's normal meal with the following amounts:

10-lb. dog
¼ cup

20-lb. dog
⅓ cup

40-lb. dog
⅔ cup

60-lb. dog
¾ cup

80-lb. dog
1 cup

100-lb. dog
1¼ cups

DESSERT FOR DINNER

Dogs definitely prefer fresh cooked chicken for their meal and for dessert. The addition of blueberries, yam, mango, and cinnamon add color, scent, and plenty of antioxidants to keep your dog healthy, even if this meal smells like a dessert.

INGREDIENTS

2 teaspoons coconut oil
2½ cups yam, cut into bite-size cubes (see page xv)
¼ teaspoon ground cinnamon
1 pound chicken breast, cut into bite-size chunks (see page xv)
½ cup blueberries
1 cup diced mango

1. Preheat the oven to 400°F. Grease a casserole dish with the oil.

2. Spread the yam chunks in the dish, and then sprinkle with the cinnamon.

3. Layer the chicken and blueberries on top of the yam, and then cover with foil or a lid.

4. Bake for 35 minutes. The yam should be very soft and the chicken cooked through.

5. Mix in the mango cubes.

Yield: 5 cups

KEY NUTRIENTS

241 calories per cup • Protein 315% • Carbohydrate-to-protein ratio 1.3 to 1 • Total fats 117% • Antioxidants 238%

Serve the following amount as a meal, twice a day:

10-lb. dog
½ to ¾ cup

20-lb. dog
¾ to 1⅓ cups

40-lb. dog
1½ to 2¼ cups

60-lb. dog
2 to 3 cups

80-lb. dog
2⅓ to 3¾ cups

100-lb. dog
2¾ to 4⅓ cups

CLUCK & QUINOA, TOO

In Feed Your Best Friend Better *I included a popular recipe for a Cluck & Quinoa casserole that is baked for an hour. Here's a new, leaner, high-protein version that's even quicker to prepare on your stovetop.*

INGREDIENTS

3 cups water
1 pound chicken breast, cut into bite-size chunks (see page xv)
1 cup uncooked quinoa
1 red bell pepper, seeded and diced
½ cup chopped carrot
½ cup chopped fresh or frozen green beans
1 clove garlic, minced

1. Bring the water to a boil in a 2-quart saucepan fitted with a lid.

2. Add the remaining ingredients and allow the mixture to return to a boil.

3. Lower the heat to low and cook for 25 minutes, stirring occasionally.

Yield: 5½ cups

KEY NUTRIENTS

229 calories per cup • Protein 355% • Carbohydrate-to-protein ratio 1 to 1 •
Total fats 115% • Antioxidants 100%

Serve the following amount as a meal, twice a day:

10-lb. dog
½ to ¾ cup

20-lb. dog
1 to 1⅓ cups

40-lb. dog
1⅔ to 2⅓ cups

60-lb. dog
2 to 3 cups

80-lb. dog
2½ to 4 cups

100-lb. dog
3 to 4⅔ cups

CHICKEN BREAST AND VEGGIES

Cutting the meat and vegetables by hand is one way to go, but I'd rather use a food processor and save time. If you cut items by hand, cut them into bite-size pieces suitable for your dog's size. Otherwise, pulse the meat in a food processor until it resembles ground meat and pulse the vegetables until they are finely chopped. Because liver tends to stick to cooking surfaces, I like to make this recipe in a nonstick skillet.

INGREDIENTS

1 tablespoon coconut or olive oil
1½ pounds chicken breast or tenders, cut into bite-size pieces (see page xv)
1 teaspoon chopped chicken liver
¼ teaspoon ground cinnamon
½ cup chopped or ground broccoli
1 cup chopped or ground carrot
1 cup chopped or ground green beans
1 red apple, cored, seeded, and chopped

1. Heat the oil in a large nonstick skillet over medium heat.

2. Add the chicken and liver, then simmer for 15 minutes, until the meat is no longer pink.

3. Sprinkle the cinnamon over the chicken.

4. Add the vegetables and apple to the skillet, then simmer 5 minutes for finely chopped vegetables or 10 minutes for larger pieces.

Yield: 6 cups

KEY NUTRIENTS

244 calories per cup • Protein 352% • Carbohydrate-to-protein ratio 0.2 to 1 • Total fats 361% • Antioxidants 225%

Serve the following amount as a meal, twice a day:

10-lb. dog
⅔ to 1 cup

20-lb. dog
1 to 1⅔ cups

40-lb. dog
2 to 2¾ cups

60-lb. dog
2⅓ to 3¾ cups

80-lb. dog
3 to 4½ cups

100-lb. dog
3⅓ to 5⅓ cups

CHICKEN COOKIES

Achieving thin, dried chicken strips is possible with a food dehydrator and plenty of patience to wait out the eight to ten hours they take to dry. This is a slightly thicker version, creating something more akin to a cookie. It's a great stuffing for a Kong because it takes longer for dogs to retrieve than soft foods and it doesn't crumble like a regular cookie.

INGREDIENTS

¼ cup coconut or olive oil

1½ pounds boneless, skinless chicken breast or tenders

1 tablespoon salt

1 tablespoon dried parsley or rosemary (do not use rosemary for dogs prone to seizures)

Ground cumin, or ground cinnamon

1. Preheat the oven to 400°F. Line a baking sheet with a silicone mat or foil. Pour the oil onto the prepared baking sheet and let it melt in the oven while you're slicing the chicken.

2. Slice the chicken lengthwise into ⅛-inch-thick strips and transfer to the baking sheet (careful, it's warm).

3. Sprinkle the chicken with the salt and your herb or spice of choice, then toss together to thoroughly mix.

4. Arrange the chicken in a single layer on the prepared baking sheet and bake for 45 minutes.

5. Flip the chicken and lower the oven temperature to 200°F. Bake the cookies for 2 hours, or until completely dry.

6. Store the chicken cookies in an airtight container in the refrigerator for up to 1 week or freeze for up to 1 month.

Yield: 40 cookies

KEY NUTRIENTS

28 calories per cookie • Protein 32% • Carbohydrate-to-protein ratio 0 to 1 • Total fats 27% • Antioxidants 7%

Daily Allowance:

10-lb. dog
1 cookie

20-lb. dog
1 cookie

40-lb. dog
2 cookies

60-lb. dog
3 cookies

80-lb. dog
4 cookies

100-lb. dog
6 cookies

CHICKEN FEET

Visiting a local pet store a few years ago, I found dried chicken feet being sold as a dog treat. We've all heard the warning about giving dogs cooked bones, so I was a little puzzled. It turns out the porous structure of bird bones that makes them more likely to splinter when cooked is actually an advantage when it comes to bird feet. The bones in the foot are incredibly thin as compared to the bones in the thigh or even the wing. When dried properly, the bones become even more brittle and with the slightest bite they turn into dust. I know because I tried one.

What really got me was the price—a buck per foot or eight dollars for a dozen. A few weekends later I saw some chicken feet at an Asian grocery store for less than two dollars for 20. I picked up a couple of packs and decided to try making the treats for my dogs. (Ask your local butcher to help you find some.)

First, you have to know that they are rather . . . aromatic. This means, right off the bat, dogs are going to love them. The cartilage and bone contain glucosamine, chondroitin, and calcium that will help maintain your dog's healthy bones and joints. Since they are covered in poultry skin, they contain about 60 percent fat, some of which can be rendered out by boiling them first. To turn them into crunchy treats, you will then need to bake the feet at a medium temperature.

After my first batch cooled, I gave some to the dogs and they were ecstatic. As long as I have the oven going, I make these in a double batch and store them in the freezer. On the plus side, by making them at home, you know there are no added preservatives or chemicals, and your dog will be jumping off all four feet for some of these treats.

CRUNCHY CHICKEN FEET

INGREDIENTS

2 pounds chicken feet (about 40)

1. Bring a large pot of water to a boil over high heat.

2. Rinse the chicken feet in cool water, drain, and transfer to the pot.

3. Allow the water to return to a boil, then lower the heat to medium-high. Cover with a lid and allow the chicken feet to simmer for 25 minutes.

4. Preheat the oven to 350°F.

5. Drain the chicken feet and discard the water. Spread out the chicken feet in a single layer on two rimmed baking sheets and transfer to the oven.

6. Bake for 1½ hours, until the treats are dark brown and break very easily when twisted.

7. Turn off the oven and allow the feet treats to cool in the oven for 1 hour.

8. Using scissors, snip off the sharp talons as you transfer the treats to an airtight container.

9. Store the treats in the refrigerator for 1 week or in the freezer for up to 3 months.

Yield: about 40 treats

KEY NUTRIENTS

Calories 10% · Protein 30% · Total fats 41% · Omega-3 (DHA) 15% · Omega 6 (LA) 36% · B_9 (folate) 49%

Daily allowance as a treat (not recommended for dogs under 20 pounds):

20-lb. dog
½ treat

40-lb. dog
1 treat

60-lb. dog
1 treat

80-lb. dog
1½ treats

100-lb. dog
2 treats

CHICKEN GIZZARDS

Let's be honest: It's doubtful chicken gizzards are making their way across the cutting board and onto the dinner plate of most American households. First off, they're chewy enough to make your jaw sore. Second is the thought of their being the "second stomach" that helps grind a chicken's food and passes it back and forth with the true stomach until the food is digestible. To accomplish all the grinding action, nature has created this muscle surrounded by a surprisingly small amount of fat, making it a very lean source of protein. Gizzards are lower in calories than even chicken breast, and just a hair higher in fat, so you can feed your dog more of this bubblegum-like meat and share high-quality protein for an economical price. Gizzards are a great supplement to commercial dry foods all on their own because they are a good source of vitamin B_3, iron, and selenium to support the immune and nervous systems.

GIMME GIZZARDS

The chewiness of chicken gizzards can be intimidating to some dogs. Sending the gizzards through the food processor reduces the amount of time you spend cooking them and the amount of time your dog has to spend chewing them.

INGREDIENTS

1 pound chicken gizzards

1. Chop the gizzards into bite-size pieces for your dog (see page xv) or grind in a food processor fitted with a cutting blade by pulsing for 30 seconds.

2. Cook the gizzards in a skillet over medium heat for 15 minutes. A light cooking is best to retain nutrients; when cooked through, the gizzards will lose their color but do not need to be browned.

Yield: 2 cups

KEY NUTRIENTS

Calories 13% • Protein 83% • Total fats 18% • Potassium 26% • Iron 38% • B$_3$ (niacin), 99% • B$_6$ (pyridoxine) 35%

1 cup of cooked gizzards has 213 calories; equivalent to about ⅔ cup of commercial dry food.

Replace one-quarter of your dog's regular meal with the following amounts:

10-lb. dog
¼ cup

20-lb. dog
⅓ cup

40-lb. dog
⅔ cup

60-lb. dog
¾ cup

80-lb. dog
1 cup

100-lb. dog
1¼ cups

GIZZARD GRIND

Using the same healthy vegetables that are found in a hearty minestrone, this grain-free, low-carb, high-protein meal doesn't need to be a lot of work, especially if you let a food processor do the majority of the work.

INGREDIENTS

2 pounds chicken gizzards
1 tablespoon coconut or olive oil
1 clove garlic, minced
1 cup kale
1 cup roughly chopped carrot
1 cup fresh or frozen green beans
½ large red bell pepper, seeded and cut into quarters
½ cup fresh or canned crushed tomatoes
Pinch of salt

1. Working in two batches, grind 1 pound of gizzards at a time in a food processor by pulsing for 30 to 45 seconds, or until they have been reduced to be slightly chunkier than ground meat.

2. Heat the oil over medium-high heat in a large skillet equipped with a lid. Add the gizzards and garlic to the skillet and lower the heat to medium. Cook the gizzards for 10 minutes, stirring occasionally to help the meat cook evenly.

3. Pulse the kale and carrot in the food processor until finely chopped and then add to the skillet. Pulse the green beans and bell pepper the same way and add to the skillet.

4. Add the tomatoes and salt to the skillet and cover the pan. Lower the heat to medium-low and simmer for 5 minutes.

Yield: 5 cups

Serve the following amount
as a meal, twice a day:

10-lb. dog
½ to ¾ cup

20-lb. dog
¾ to 1⅓ cups

40-lb. dog
1½ to 2 cups

60-lb. dog
2 to 3 cups

80-lb. dog
2⅓ to 3⅔ cups

100-lb. dog
2¾ to 4⅓ cups

KEY NUTRIENTS

245 calories per cup • Protein 487% • Carbohydrate-to-protein ratio 0.3 to 1 • Total fats 178% • Antioxidants 185%

GIZZARDS PORRIDGE

Want to surprise your dog? This meal looks like a porridge, but inside are chewy chunks of gizzard . . . and healthy kale and apples that your pet won't even notice.

INGREDIENTS

2 tablespoons coconut or olive oil
1 clove garlic, minced
2 cups water
½ pound boneless, skinless chicken thighs
½ pound chicken gizzards
½ cup millet
1 cup chopped kale
1 cup cored and chopped red apple

1. Heat the oil in a 2-quart saucepan over medium-high heat.

2. Add the garlic and sauté for 1 minute.

3. Stir in the water, chicken, gizzards, and millet and allow the pot to return to a boil.

4. Lower the heat to low, cover, and cook for 30 minutes, stirring occasionally. The millet should be thick and soft.

5. Remove from the heat and stir in the kale and apple.

Yield: 5 cups

KEY NUTRIENTS

241 calories per cup • Protein 285% • Carbohydrate-to-protein ratio 1 to 1 •
Total fats 243% • Antioxidants 180%

Serve the following amount as a meal, twice a day:

10-lb. dog
½ to ¾ cup

20-lb. dog
¾ to 1⅓ cups

40-lb. dog
1½ to 2¼ cups

60-lb. dog
2 to 3 cups

80-lb. dog
2⅓ to 3¾ cups

100-lb. dog
2¾ to 4⅓ cups

CHICKEN HEARTS

A look of confusion and concern enters a dog's face when she experiences a serious illness. There might be a whimper, hinting at pain, or maybe a low grumble while settling into bed. At regular intervals your pet will hear the rattle of a prescription bottle and tense up for the contest of wills. Eventually peanut butter will fail to convince and even the scent of cheese won't be able to hide the chemical scent of a prescription meant to heal and comfort. A talented tongue can somehow manage to clean the good parts off the drugs and spit out the bitter pills. Other dogs will just spit out the whole package. As each pill begins to dissolve, your struggle becomes more desperate and your dog's resolve to not swallow it becomes even stronger.

Pill pockets are rather expensive and filled with sweeteners and artificial ingredients, making them just as unhealthy as the cheese or peanut butter you were using to bribe. Nature provides a better option in the form of the universal sign for love: the heart. Except this one has no resemblance to a valentine and it comes from a chicken.

Yup, the chicken heart. And while they often can be found in a whole chicken packaged with giblets, chicken hearts can also be purchased all on their own.

The chicken heart has a natural opening: one of the arteries at the tip of the organ. Tuck a pill into one of these and your dog will never be the wiser. She won't know the chicken heart is also providing protein, vitamins B_6 (pyridoxine), B_9 (folate), and B_{12} (cyanocobalamin) to assist the body in the manufacturing all the necessary proteins, hormones, and red blood cells need to return it to full health. If your dog is not eating much, the chicken hearts will definitely tempt her, and the broth will also provide nourishment and hydration.

The secret to a successful pill delivery lies not only in hiding the pill but also in playing the shell game with your dog. I tend to give the hearts in a series of three: The first chicken heart primes the pump and gets the dog excited, the second hides the pill, and the expectation of the third gives the dog a reason to rush to swallow the second one.

It's not difficult to show your ailing dog how much you care; just give her a little heart.

POULTRY PILL POCKETS

This recipe is a must for when dogs need to take medicine, but it's also an easy treat that you can make anytime. In our house it's also a training treat.

INGREDIENTS

1 pound chicken hearts (about 50 hearts)
4 cups water

1. Bring the chicken hearts and water to a boil in a 2-quart saucepan.

2. Lower the heat to medium-low and simmer for 15 minutes

3. Drain the stock and reserve for pouring over your dog's food or using in any recipe calling for chicken stock.

Yield: about 50 treats, 14 calories each

KEY NUTRIENTS

Calories 15% • Protein 52% • Total fats 57% • Carbohydrates 1 g • Iron 65% • Zinc 36% • B_3 (niacin) 94% • B_5 (pantothenic acid) 57% • B_6 (pyridoxine) 81% • B_9 (folate) 89% • B_{12} (cyanocobalamin) 69%

Daily portion as treats or as pill pockets:

10-lb. dog
4 hearts

20-lb. dog
6 hearts

40-lb. dog
10 hearts

60-lb. dog
15 hearts

80-lb. dog
18 hearts

100-lb. dog
21 hearts

CHICKEN LIVER

Someday, when dogs learn to use the Internet, there will be complete websites devoted to chicken liver. It will be the most "liked" page on Facebook, with every posting receiving millions of tail-wag "likes." Humans have ice cream, cookies, pies, and cakes—for dogs, the preferred dessert is chicken liver.

While not quite a junk food, chicken liver should be fed in moderation because of the high amounts of certain nutrients. In man, dog, or fowl, the liver's purpose is to detoxify the body, synthesize biochemicals needed for digestion, and store vitamins in the body for later use. When liver is included as part of the diet, it has both benefits and drawbacks. Chicken liver is far richer in vitamin A than any other type of chicken meat, with a whopping 50,000 milligrams in a pound of liver and a mere 113 milligrams in equal weight of chicken breast or thighs. Vitamin A nourishes everything from the eyes to the heart and skin; it also acts as an antioxidant and contributes to the fight against cancer. However, when there is an excess, it'll be stored in your dog's own liver. An excess of vitamin A can cause constipation, a lack of appetite, or lameness. Liver can also have the opposite effect of causing loose stools, which is why I don't use liver as a training treat.

Chicken liver is not necessarily a bad food for dogs; it just needs to be used with a fair amount of moderation. Just what you and I might need to practice with ice cream.

FRIED CHICKEN LIVER

Liver is rarely sold in portions less than a pound, so for me the best thing to do is cook it as soon as I get home and then freeze it in a plastic freezer bag. You can break off a frozen piece much easier after the liver has been cooked than when it's frozen raw. This way, whether you want to use it for a little nutritional boost for your dog's bowl or as a treat, it's easily accessible. Cooking in a nonstick pan is essential when dealing with the sticking power of liver.

If you find yourself stealing a few chicken livers (they are great spread on lightly toasted bread), just be sure the dog doesn't catch you.

INGREDIENTS

1 pound chicken livers

1. Spread out the chicken livers in a nonstick pan and cook over medium heat for 10 minutes, breaking the livers into pieces with a spatula as they cook.

2. Turn the livers over and cook for 10 more minutes, until lightly browned and crumbly.

3. Let the livers cool and then give your patient dog a little treat before transferring the rest to a plastic freezer bag.

4. Lay the bag on a flat surface in the freezer until they are frozen. A thin layer will allow you to break off pieces much more easily.

Yield: 1½ cups

KEY NUTRIENTS

Calories 3% • Protein 15% • Total fats 8% • Carbohydrates 0.32 g • Iron 27% • A 198% • B_9 (folate) 197% • B_{12} (cyanocobalamin) 43%

---

1 chicken liver has 52 calories; equivalent to about 2 tablespoons of commercial dry food.

Portion sizes for supplementing commercial dry foods 2 to 3 times a week, rather than daily:*

10-lb. dog
⅛ teaspoon

20-lb. dog
¼ teaspoon

40-lb. dog
¼ teaspoon

60-lb. dog
½ teaspoon

80-lb. dog
1 teaspoon

100-lb. dog
1½ teaspoons

*Dogs with liver disease should not be fed foods rich in vitamin A.

THE CHICKEN LIVER CHEAT

To tempt dogs into trying new foods or just adding extra vitamins and minerals from chicken liver, sprinkle a little dehydrated chicken liver on your dog's meals.

INGREDIENTS

1 pound chicken livers

1. Preheat the oven to 400°F. Line a baking sheet with a silicone sheet or parchment paper to prevent the liver from sticking.

2. In either a small bowl or the container in which you purchased the chicken livers, snip at the livers with kitchen scissors to make pieces smaller than ½ inch. Spread the liver across the baking sheet so the pieces are spaced slightly apart.

3. Bake for 45 minutes. You may hear an occasional popping sound as water escapes from the liver.

4. Turn off the oven and allow the livers to rest in the oven for 30 to 60 minutes. The livers need to be very dry.

5. Transfer the liver to a food processor fitted with a chopping blade, or a blender, and chop until the liver is reduced to a fine dust. If making a larger batch, chop only 1 cup at a time to get the finest powder.

6. Sprinkle some in your dog's dish to try it out. Store the rest of the liver powder in an airtight container in the freezer for up to 6 months.

Yield: ⅔ cup

KEY NUTRIENTS

Calories 1% • Protein 5% • Total fats 3% • Iron 9% • A 63% • B_9 (folate) 63%

Treat-size portions, to be served a maximum of 2 or 3 times per week:

10-lb. dog
⅛ teaspoon

20-lb. dog
¼ teaspoon

40-lb. dog
¼ teaspoon

60-lb. dog
½ teaspoon

80-lb. dog
1 teaspoon

100-lb. dog
1½ teaspoons

WAYS TO USE THE CHICKEN LIVER CHEAT:

• Stir ½ teaspoon into any finished meal recipe in this book.

• Combine ¼ teaspoon with 2 tablespoons of low-fat cream cheese or ricotta as a treat in a Kong.

• Rub a little on your hands when dealing with a shy dog. It's weird, but it works.

• For dogs with kennel cough, make them a natural cough syrup: Chicken Liver Cough Syrup (page 46).

CHICKEN LIVER COUGH SYRUP

Unfortunately, even with vaccination, a day at doggy daycare occasionally results in a dog contracting kennel cough. Antibiotics may be prescribed, but even then symptoms usually last for around a week. The ginger and turmeric in this home remedy will fight inflammation, while the vinegar and honey soothe the throat and kill bacteria. The Chicken Liver Cheat is in there just to say "get well soon."

INGREDIENTS

3 tablespoons grated fresh ginger (see note)
2 tablespoons ground turmeric
2 tablespoons honey
2 tablespoons apple cider vinegar
⅓ cup hot water
½ teaspoon Chicken Liver Cheat (page 46)

1. Place all the ingredients in a bowl and mix thoroughly to combine. Store the cough syrup in an airtight container in the refrigerator for up to 1 week.

Yield: 1 cup

Note: Grate the ginger with a Microplane grater. Or using two forks: Pierce the ginger at one end with a fork, and hold the fork upright to keep the ginger stationary. With another fork, rake at the ginger from the opposite end, working your way toward the first fork. Repeat until you have about 3 tablespoons of grated ginger.

Daily allowance, split into multiple servings mixed into your dog's meals:

10-lb. dog
1¼ teaspoons

20-lb. dog
2 teaspoons

40-lb. dog
3½ teaspoons

60-lb. dog
5 teaspoons

80-lb. dog
2 tablespoons

100-lb. dog
3 tablespoons

CHICKEN THIGHS

When it comes to making my own dinner, I much prefer to use chicken thighs rather than chicken breasts. With the same weight of both varying in calories by less than 1 percent, my preference leans toward taste. However, there is a trade-off in nutritional content, with slightly less protein in the thighs and over 50 percent more fat. Thighs are not a bad choice for meals; we just need to balance out the fat with other ingredients.

The story continues to change if you include the skin. The fat content of thighs with skin is four times that of skinless thighs and more than six times as high as that of skinless chicken breast, with only two-thirds of the protein.

For homemade meals, I recommend using skinless thighs because a moderate amount of fat is important to your dog for the health of the immune system and just about every cell in the body. Fatty acids are also an important source of energy and enable the body to store the fat-soluble vitamins A, D, E and K.

On a diet of commercial foods, your dog is already getting an average of 215 percent of his needed fat; if you're adding any type of fat, it would be best in the form of fish oil for its omega-3 fatty acids or coconut oil for its beneficial properties. Chicken breasts, tenders, gizzards, and hearts are leaner and therefore a better choice than thighs to balance out the fat in commercial dry foods and increase the amount of quality protein in your dog's diet.

How best to use chicken thighs:

- *Primarily in meat-based homemade foods*: Skinless thighs will add both an appropriate amount of fats and protein. For dogs needing to lose weight, definitely consider using half skinless thighs and half chicken tenders (or another lean cut of meat).

- *If homemade foods contain 50 percent or more grain (1 pound of meat to 1 cup of grain)*: Grains are much lower in fat than meat is, so including a few of the skins from the thighs will ensure your dog is receiving enough fat in his diet. Use no more than one skin from every five thighs.

MEAL-TOPPING THIGHS

Somebody will be wagging her tail when you provide something so simple yet so desirable. Cooking over medium heat in a nonstick skillet means you don't have to add any fat, and cleanup will be a cinch.

INGREDIENTS

1 pound boneless, skinless chicken thighs (about 4 thighs)
¼ teaspoon garlic powder (optional)

1. Spread a single layer of chicken thighs in a nonstick skillet over medium heat and sprinkle with the garlic powder.

2. Cook for 10 minutes, then turn over and cook for 10 to 12 more minutes, so the chicken thighs are cooked through.

3. Allow the chicken to cool, then cut into bite-size chunks for your dog (see page xv).

Yield: 2 cups

KEY NUTRIENTS

Calories 17% • Protein 92% • Total fats 35% • Omega-3 (ALA) 33% • Phosphorus 28% • Potassium 27% • B$_3$ (niacin) 150% • B$_6$ (pyridoxine) 141%

Replace one-third of your dog's regular meal with the following amounts:

10-lb. dog
¼ cup

20-lb. dog
⅓ cup

40-lb. dog
⅔ cup

60-lb. dog
¾ cup

80-lb. dog
1 cup

100-lb. dog
1¼ cups

MOROCCAN FOR MUTTS

If you're making couscous for yourself, why not bring a little Moroccan flavor to your dog's bowl, too? This dish will entice your pet's nose with its heady scent as well as provide a hefty helping of antioxidants from many of the same ingredients that go into the side dishes you pair with your couscous.

INGREDIENTS

1 tablespoon olive or coconut oil
1 pound boneless, skinless chicken thighs, diced
1 clove garlic, minced (optional)
1 cup fresh or canned crushed tomatoes
1 cup chopped broccoli
1 cup chopped carrot
1 (15.5-ounce) can garbanzo beans, drained and rinsed
¼ teaspoon ground cinnamon

1. Heat the oil in a large skillet over medium heat.

2. Add the chicken and cook for 20 minutes, stirring occasionally, until lightly browned.

3. Stir in the garlic (if using) and cook for 3 minutes.

4. Add the remaining ingredients, stir to combine, and cook for 10 minutes. Mash the garbanzo beans with the back of a spoon so they absorb more of the chicken flavor and are more enticing and easier for your dog to eat.

Yield: 4½ cups

KEY NUTRIENTS

264 calories per cup • Protein 336% • Carbohydrate-to-protein ratio 0.8 to 1 •
Total fats 215% • Antioxidants 205%

Serve the following amount as a meal, twice a day:

10-lb. dog
½ to ¾ cup

20-lb. dog
¾ to 1¼ cups

40-lb. dog
1⅓ to 2 cups

60-lb. dog
1⅔ to 2¾ cups

80-lb. dog
2¼ to 3½ cups

100-lb. dog
2½ to 4 cups

CHICKEN THIGHS, SQUASH, & SPROUTS

Roasting squash for your own dinner will get the oven going, and as long as it's hot, you can cook a simple dish for your dog right alongside it. Layering the chicken on top of the squash and sprouts and cooking for an hour gives the vegetables the ability to soak up the chicken flavor in this dish. If there is a little extra juice left in the pan, pour the extra flavor over the food!

INGREDIENTS

1 tablespoon olive or coconut oil
1 cup chopped Brussels sprouts
4 cups seeded and diced butternut squash (1½ pounds)
1 red bell pepper, seeded and diced
1 pound boneless, skinless chicken thighs, diced
1 cup chicken stock
½ teaspoon ground turmeric
2 teaspoons nutritional yeast

1. Preheat the oven to 350°F. Grease an 8-inch square baking dish with the oil.

2. Spread the Brussels sprouts in a single layer across the bottom of the dish, then cover with the butternut squash, bell pepper, chicken, chicken stock, and turmeric.

3. Cover with foil and cook for 1 hour, or until the butternut squash is tender.

4. Remove from the oven and sprinkle with the nutritional yeast.

Yield: 6 cups

KEY NUTRIENTS

190 calories per cup • Protein 326% • Carbohydrate-to-protein ratio 1 to 1 • Total fats 203% • Antioxidants 209%

Serve the following amount as a meal, twice a day:

10-lb. dog
⅔ to 1 cup

20-lb. dog
1 to 1⅔ cups

40-lb. dog
1¾ to 2¾ cups

60-lb. dog
2⅓ to 3¾ cups

80-lb. dog
3 to 4¾ cups

100-lb. dog
3½ to 5½ cups

QUICK CHICKEN & OATS

Chicken provides a savory flavor your dog will enjoy and the oats provide a full stomach to keep your pet dozing in her favorite sunny patch—probably dreaming about the next meal.

INGREDIENTS

3 cups water
1 pound boneless, skinless chicken thighs, diced
1 cup rolled oats
½ cup seeded and chopped red bell pepper
1 cup chopped kale
1 teaspoon nutritional yeast

1. Bring the water to a boil in a 2-quart saucepan.

2. Add the chicken and lower the heat to medium. Allow the chicken to simmer for 15 minutes.

3. Stir in the oats, bell pepper, and kale and cover tightly with a lid. Lower the heat to low and cook for 10 minutes, or until the oats have fully absorbed the water.

Yield: 4½ cups

KEY NUTRIENTS

270 calories per cup • Protein 342% • Carbohydrate-to-protein ratio 1 to 1 • Total fats 158% • Antioxidants 59%

Serve the following amount as a meal, twice a day:

10-lb. dog
½ to ¾ cup

20-lb. dog
¾ to 1¼ cups

40-lb. dog
1⅓ to 2 cups

60-lb. dog
1⅔ to 2¾ cups

80-lb. dog
2¼ to 3½ cups

100-lb. dog
2½ to 4 cups

GROUND CHICKEN & VEGETABLES

This meal has a high meat content because it's combined with low-calorie vegetables and just a bit of cooking fat. Whether you're making tacos or chicken burgers, pick up some extra ground chicken to share with your dog.

INGREDIENTS

1 tablespoon coconut or olive oil
1 cup cored and diced (½-inch) apple
½ cup frozen spinach, thawed
½ cup chopped carrots
½ cup chopped broccoli
1½ pounds 85% lean ground chicken

1. Preheat the oven to 400°F.

2. Grease a baking dish with the oil and pile in the apple and vegetables.

3. Crumble the chicken over the top and cover with foil

4. Bake for 40 minutes, or until the vegetables have softened and the chicken is cooked through.

Yield: 5 cups

KEY NUTRIENTS

241 calories per cup • Protein 353% • Carbohydrate-to-protein ratio 0.2 to 1 •
Total fats 365% • Antioxidants 180%

Serve the following amount
as a meal, twice a day:

10-lb. dog
½ to ¾ cup

20-lb. dog
¾ to 1⅓ cups

40-lb. dog
1½ to 2¼ cups

60-lb. dog
2 to 3 cups

80-lb. dog
2⅓ to 3¾ cups

100-lb. dog
2¾ to 4⅓ cups

GROUND CHICKEN, PEARS, & QUINOA

Pears are great in tarts for the table or made into pear butter for toast. However, they are just as good as part of a savory dinner for your dog. The great taste of chicken is combined with the sweet flavor of pears, with just a bit of quinoa to soak up all the flavorful juices. Chicken stock is used rather than water, to add even more flavor and to round out the calories. If you'd like to make a version with water, it will lower the calories, fat, and protein by 8 percent.

INGREDIENTS

1½ cups chicken stock or bone broth (page 25)
1 pound ground chicken
½ cup uncooked quinoa
1 cup chopped green beans
1 red Anjou pear

1. Combine the stock, chicken, and quinoa in a 2-quart saucepan and bring to a simmer over high heat.

2. Lower the heat to low, add the green beans, and simmer for 25 minutes.

3. Remove from the heat and allow the chicken mixture to cool.

4. Stem and core the pear, then chop it into ½-inch dice; you can leave the skin on if you purchased organic; otherwise, remove and discard the peel.

5. Stir the pear into the chicken mixture.

Yield: 5 cups

KEY NUTRIENTS

240 calories per cup • Protein 271% • Carbohydrate-to-protein ratio 0.9 to 1 • Total fats 223% • Antioxidants 127%

Serve the following amount as a meal, twice a day:

10-lb. dog
½ to ¾ cup

20-lb. dog
¾ to 1⅓ cups

40-lb. dog
1½ to 2¼ cups

60-lb. dog
2 to 3 cups

80-lb. dog
2⅓ to 3¾ cups

100-lb. dog
2¾ to 4⅓ cups

CHICKEN & RUTABAGA

Starting with the rutabaga allows the other flavors to drift downward and be absorbed by the rutabaga. I like to chop the broccoli finely and then cook it for a brief time so it softens but doesn't lose all the important nutrients.

INGREDIENTS

1 tablespoon coconut or olive oil
1 pound rutabaga, peeled and cut into 1-inch dice
1 clove garlic, minced
1 pound ground chicken
1 cup finely chopped broccoli

1. Preheat the oven to 400°F.

2. Grease an 8-inch square baking dish with the oil, then layer in the rutabaga, garlic, and chicken.

3. Cover with a lid or foil and bake for 30 minutes. The rutabaga should almost be tender; if not, bake for 5 more minutes.

4. Stir in the broccoli and bake for 10 minutes; the broccoli should be soft and the rutabaga tender.

Yield: 5 cups

KEY NUTRIENTS

243 calories per cup • Protein 276% • Carbohydrate-to-protein ratio 1 to 1 • Total fats 273% • Antioxidants 29%

Serve the following amount as a meal, twice a day:

10-lb. dog
½ to ¾ cup

20-lb. dog
¾ to 1⅓ cups

40-lb. dog
1½ to 2¼ cups

60-lb. dog
2 to 3 cups

80-lb. dog
2⅓ to 3¾ cups

100-lb. dog
2¾ to 4⅓ cups

TURKEY

Well-intentioned sharing at Thanksgiving has given turkey a bad reputation among dog owners. The day after Thanksgiving is a very busy time for veterinarian offices and animal emergency hospitals because dogs given turkey skin and other rich foods end up with serious digestive problems. Turkey skin is high in fat, and if you're like many people, you're basting the turkey skin in fat so the bird comes to the table golden brown and crispy. As delicious as it is, it's not something we should share with our four-legged family members. In the worst cases it can cause acute pancreatitis; the pancreas normally functions to help produce enzymes crucial to the digestion of proteins, carbohydrates, and fats, but faced with an overload of fat, it becomes inflamed. If your dog has been given turkey skin and appears to be lethargic, or is vomiting or having diarrhea, it's worth putting off Black Friday shopping to have your pet examined.

Turkey can safely be incorporated into your dog's meal with the following guidelines:

- *Turkey breast*: Take the skin off the turkey breast and it's 45 percent lower in fat than chicken breast.

- *Turkey thighs*: Turkey thighs without the skin are actually lower in fat and higher in protein than skinless chicken thighs, with 10 percent fewer calories overall.

- *85% lean ground turkey*: A good mixture for mixing with starchy vegetables or grain.

- *90% lean ground turkey*: If you're avoiding carbohydrates for your dog, 90% lean provides a good balance of fat and protein.

When buying ground turkey, if it's not clearly labeled with the fat percentage, leave it on the shelf. Often rolls of turkey look like a good deal, but if they are loaded with greater than 15 percent fat, the end result could be a visit to the veterinarian.

TIME FOR TURKEY

Most of us reserve cooking a big turkey for Thanksgiving, but for your dog you can make turkey anytime, by buying it ground. Instead of annually, why not make this a monthly tradition?

INGREDIENTS

½ pound 90% lean ground turkey
¼ teaspoon dried oregano (omit for dogs prone to seizures)
1 clove garlic, minced

1. Crumble the turkey into a nonstick skillet and sprinkle with the oregano and garlic.

2. Heat over medium heat and cook the turkey for 15 minutes, stirring occasionally.

Yield: 1 cup

KEY NUTRIENTS

Calories 16% • Protein 69% • Total fats 49% • Omega-3 (ALA) 85% •
Omega 6 (LA) 62% • Sodium 25% • B_3 (niacin) 136% • B_6 (pyridoxine) 133%

1 cup of ground turkey has 336 calories; equivalent to about 1 cup of commercial dry food.

Replace one-third of your dog's regular meal with the following amounts:

10-lb. dog
3 tablespoons

20-lb. dog
⅓ cup

40-lb. dog
½ cup

60-lb. dog
⅔ cup

80-lb. dog
¾ cup

100-lb. dog
1 cup

LEAN TURKEY & LENTILS

It doesn't get leaner than turkey breast; in fact, it's so lean we need to add a little coconut oil to meet your dog's minimum recommended daily requirement for fats. Combining the turkey with lentils packs this meal with protein, and is easy to prepare alongside a delicious lentil soup for you. Meanwhile, the turmeric and cinnamon provide a powerful antioxidant and cancer-fighting punch as well as make your kitchen smell really great. If your dog needs to lose a few pounds, this is the meal to help trim him down while still maintaining lean muscle mass.

INGREDIENTS

¾ cup dried lentils (black, red, green, or brown are all good choices)
1 tablespoon coconut or olive oil
1 pound turkey breast
½ cup frozen spinach, thawed
1 cup chopped cauliflower
¼ teaspoon ground cinnamon
1 teaspoon ground turmeric
2 cups water

1. Spread the lentils on a plate and discard any small rocks or debris you find.

2. Heat the oil in a large, heavy skillet over medium heat.

3. Add the turkey and brown lightly, breaking up the turkey with a spatula, about 10 minutes.

4. Add the remaining ingredients and cover the pan with a lid. Cook for 25 minutes. The lentils should be very soft and the water almost completely absorbed.

Yield: 5 cups

KEY NUTRIENTS

227 calories per cup • Protein 430% • Carbohydrate-to-protein ratio 0.7 to 1 •
Total fats 131% • Antioxidants 611%

Serve the following amount as a meal, twice a day:

10-lb. dog
½ to ¾ cup

20-lb. dog
¾ to 1⅓ cups

40-lb. dog
1⅔ to 2⅓ cups

60-lb. dog
2 to 3¼ cups

80-lb. dog
2½ to 4 cups

100-lb. dog
3 to 4⅔ cups

QUICK TURKEY QUINOA

This meal can be prepared with only about 10 minutes of active effort on your part to chop the vegetables and give the pot the occasional stir.

INGREDIENTS

½ cup frozen spinach, thawed
2½ cups water
½ cup chopped carrot
¼ cup chopped fresh parsley
1 pound 85% lean ground turkey
1 cup uncooked quinoa

1. Place the spinach and water in a 2-quart saucepan and bring to a boil over high heat.

2. Stir all the remaining ingredients into the saucepan.

3. Allow the water to return to a boil, then lower the heat to low. Simmer for 30 minutes, or until the quinoa has absorbed all the water.

Yield: 5 cups

KEY NUTRIENTS

239 calories per cup • Protein 322% • Carbohydrate-to-protein ratio 0.8 to 1 • Total fats 229% • Antioxidants 60%

Serve the following amount as a meal, twice a day:

10-lb. dog
½ to ¾ cup

20-lb. dog
¾ to 1⅓ cups

40-lb. dog
1½ to 2¼ cups

60-lb. dog
2 to 3 cups

80-lb. dog
2⅓ to 3¾ cups

100-lb. dog
2¾ to 4⅓ cups

TURKEY, YAM, & KALE

When you pull this out of the oven and uncover it, your dog will come running. The yams and cumin will help alleviate inflammation so that each time you make it, your dog might be running a little faster.

INGREDIENTS

3 cups cubed yam
1 teaspoon dried oregano (omit for dogs prone to seizures)
1 teaspoon ground cumin
2 cups chopped kale
1 pound 85% lean ground turkey

1. Preheat the oven to 400°F.

2. Spread the yam cubes across the bottom of an 8-inch square baking dish.

3. Sprinkle the oregano and cumin over the yam.

4. Spread the kale over the yam and then crumble the turkey on top of the kale.

5. Cover with a lid or foil and bake for 35 minutes, or until yam is soft and the turkey is cooked through.

Yield: 5 cups

KEY NUTRIENTS

239 calories per cup • Protein 322% • Carbohydrate-to-protein ratio 1.3 to 1 •
Total fats 229% • Antioxidants 60%

Serve the following amount as a meal, twice a day:

10-lb. dog
½ to ¾ cup

20-lb. dog
¾ to 1⅓ cups

40-lb. dog
1½ to 2¼ cups

60-lb. dog
2 to 3 cups

80-lb. dog
2⅓ to 3¾ cups

100-lb. dog
2¾ to 4⅓ cups

TURKEY & VEGGIE SIMMER

If you would like to reverse the carbohydrate-to-protein ratio in your dog's favor, this quick-simmering dish makes it easy while supplying a wide variety of antioxidants through low-calorie and low-carbohydrate vegetables.

INGREDIENTS

1½ pounds 85% lean ground turkey
1 teaspoon grated fresh ginger
1 cup chopped kale
1 cup chopped carrot
1 cup chopped green beans
1 cup seeded and chopped red bell pepper
1 cup water

1. Combine the turkey and ginger in a large skillet and cook over medium heat until lightly browned, about 5 minutes.

2. Stir the vegetables and water into the turkey mixture. When the water begins to simmer, lower the heat to low and cook for 15 minutes, until the vegetables are softened.

Yield: 6 cups

KEY NUTRIENTS

197 calories per cup • Protein 416% • Carbohydrate-to-protein ratio 0.2 to 1 • Total fats 288% • Antioxidants 137%

Serve the following amount as a meal, twice a day:

10-lb. dog
⅔ to 1 cup

20-lb. dog
1 to 1⅔ cups

40-lb. dog
2 to 2¾ cups

60-lb. dog
2⅓ to 3⅔ cups

80-lb. dog
3 to 4½ cups

100-lb. dog
3⅓ to 5⅓ cups

LAMB

"Gamey" is what many people say about lamb when they find the taste and scent a little too strong for their palate. "I'm game" is what dogs say when you provide them with this tasty meat. There is quite a difference between domestic lamb and lamb from New Zealand or Australia. Domestic lambs usually start out being fed grass but are later switched to grain to fatten them up. Lambs sourced abroad mostly live outdoors and are maintained on a diet of grass, resulting in slightly leaner meat. While I generally prefer to purchase domestic products, New Zealand or Australian lamb also has the benefit of being higher in conjugated linoleic acid (CLA), a recently discovered beneficial fat. CLA is three to five times higher in the meat of grass-fed animals and is known to be an effective fighter against various cancers in all stages of cancer development.

Ground lamb has about the same amount of protein and fat as 80% lean ground beef. It's a pretty hefty amount of fat, so I usually use it in combination with other foods to make a leaner meal.

LET ME HAVE THE LAMB—MEAL TOPPER

Sure it's fatty, but fat is also what makes lamb so delicious. When making lamb burgers for your dinner, go ahead and share it with your dog, just in a small amount. Adding a little water makes this a little saucier and helps spread the flavor around the rest of the meal.

INGREDIENTS

½ pound ground lamb
1 clove garlic, minced
1 teaspoon minced fresh rosemary (omit for dogs prone to seizures)
¼ cup water

1. Crumble the lamb into a nonstick skillet and sprinkle with the garlic and rosemary.

2. Cook over medium heat for 12 minutes, stirring occasionally.

3. Add the water and simmer for 3 minutes more.

Yield: ¾ cup

KEY NUTRIENTS

Calories 10% • Protein 19% • Total fats 50% • B₃ (niacin) 40%

1 cup of ground lamb has 640 calories; equivalent to about 1¾ cups of commercial dry food.

Replace one-fifth of your dog's regular meal with the following amounts:

10-lb. dog
2 tablespoons

20-lb. dog
2 tablespoons

40-lb. dog
3 tablespoons

60-lb. dog
¼ cup

80-lb. dog
¼ cup

100-lb. dog
⅓ cup

LAMB HASH

By the time this is done cooking, your dog won't know there are turnips inside because it will just taste like lamb, as the turnips absorb the meaty juices.

INGREDIENTS

2 cups water
4 cups peeled and chopped parsnip (1¼ pounds)
½ pound ground lamb
½ cup chopped carrot
1 cup chopped fresh or frozen green beans
1 clove garlic, minced
¼ cup fresh parsley

1. In a large skillet, bring the water to a boil.

2. Add the parsnip and allow the water to return to a boil.

3. Crumble the lamb over the parsnip, then add the garlic, carrot, and green beans.

4. Lower the heat to medium, cover the skillet, and cook for 35 minutes, or until most of the water has evaporated.

Yield: 5 cups

KEY NUTRIENTS

230 calories per cup • Protein 144% • Carbohydrate-to-protein ratio 2.5 to 1 • Total fats 305% • Antioxidants 131%

Serve the following amount as a meal, twice a day:

10-lb. dog
½ to ¾ cup

20-lb. dog
1 to 1⅓ cups

40-lb. dog
1⅔ to 2⅓ cups

60-lb. dog
2 to 3 cups

80-lb. dog
2½ to 4 cups

100-lb. dog
3 to 4⅔ cups

LAMB IN THE BARLEY

You can cut the fattiness of the lamb by combining it with barley, then boost the nutrition by adding some Swiss chard (or an equal amount of other greens) with this simple recipe.

INGREDIENTS

2 cups water

1 cup canned crushed tomatoes

¾ cup barley (hulled barley is more nutritious than pearled barley, but either is fine)

½ pound ground lamb

1 cup chopped Swiss chard

1. Combine all the ingredients in a 2-quart saucepan and bring to a boil.

2. Lower the heat to low and simmer for 1 hour, or until the barley has absorbed all the moisture and is very tender.

Yield: 4 cups

KEY NUTRIENTS

314 calories per cup • Protein 158% • Carbohydrate-to-protein ratio 2.4 to 1 • Total fats 280% • Antioxidants 68%

Serve the following amount as a meal, twice a day:

10-lb. dog
½ to ¾ cup

20-lb. dog
1 to 1⅓ cups

40-lb. dog
1⅔ to 2⅓ cups

60-lb. dog
2 to 3 cups

80-lb. dog
2½ to 4 cups

100-lb. dog
3 to 4⅔ cups

AD HOC LAMB STEW

Lamb neck bones aren't a good treat for your dog to gnaw on, but they can make a quick and easy stew. Since they have a lot of remaining meat but need some help to let the meat fall off the bone, a long simmer will help out. Roasting the bones enhances the flavor and helps some of the fat render out of the meat, making this dish a little leaner.

INGREDIENTS

2 pounds lamb neck bones

4 cups roughly chopped vegetables (feel free to use any vegetables mentioned in this book)

1 sprig rosemary (omit for dogs prone to seizures)

1 teaspoon dried cumin, oregano (avoid oregano for dogs prone to seizures), or thyme

½ teaspoon ground cinnamon

1 quart water

1. Preheat the oven to 400°F.

2. Spread the lamb bones on a rimmed baking sheet and roast for 25 minutes. The meat should be slightly cooked and the bones will be richly colored, even blackened in some places.

3. Combine the bones, vegetables, and your herb or spice of choice in a large stockpot. Add water to cover the bones and vegetables.

4. Bring to a boil over high heat, then lower the heat to low. Simmer for 90 minutes up to 2 hours; longer cooking will enhance flavor and the nutrients will leach into the broth, in addition to making the lamb meat easier to remove from the bone.

5. Place a large colander over a large bowl and strain the stew, reserving the broth.

6. Remove and discard the bones and chop the meat in appropriately sized chunks for your dog (see page xv). When you

Serve the following amount as a meal, twice a day:

10-lb. dog
⅓ to ¾ cup

20-lb. dog
¾ to 1 cup

40-lb. dog
1⅓ to 2 cups

60-lb. dog
1⅔ to 2½ cups

80-lb. dog
2 to 3 cups

100-lb. dog
2⅓ to 3¾ cups

think you've found all the bones, check one more time just to be sure.

7. Skim the fat off the broth. Recombine the meat and vegetables with the broth and serve!

Yield: 5 cups

KEY NUTRIENTS

281 calories per cup • Protein 178% • Carbohydrate-to-protein ratio 1.6 to 1 • Total fats 329% • Antioxidants 138%

LAMB & LENTILS

Since ground lamb can be fatty, this recipe balances the fat out by using lentils to provide both additional protein and some grain-free carbohydrates. Make a whole batch of lentils for yourself and add what's left over to this recipe.

INGREDIENTS

¾ cup dried lentils
1½ cups water
⅓ pound ground lamb
½ cup chopped tomatoes
1 clove garlic
½ teaspoon ground turmeric
¼ teaspoon ground cinnamon
1 cup chopped kale

1. Spread the lentils on a plate and discard any small rocks or debris you find.

2. Combine the lentils, water, lamb, tomatoes, garlic, and spices in a 2-quart saucepan, stirring the ingredients to fully break up and distribute the ground lamb.

3. Bring to a simmer over medium-high heat and then lower the heat to low. Cover and cook for 30 minutes.

4. Stir the kale into the mixture and remove the saucepan from the heat. Cover and allow the kale to wilt from the heat of the lamb and lentils, about 5 minutes.

Yield: 3½ cups

KEY NUTRIENTS

348 calories per cup • Protein 228% • Carbohydrate-to-protein ratio 1.3 to 1 •
Total fats 289% • Antioxidants 492%

Serve the following amount
as a meal, twice a day:

10-lb. dog
⅓ to ½ cup

20-lb. dog
⅔ to 1 cup

40-lb. dog
1 to 1½ cups

60-lb. dog
1⅓ to 2 cups

80-lb. dog
1⅔ to 2½ cups

100-lb. dog
2 to 3 cups

PORK

Many commercial dog foods go beyond beef, chicken, and turkey to offer duck, rabbit, venison, and salmon, but one of the most underutilized meats is pork. Generally easier on your pocketbook than most other meats, the lean cuts of pork can also be easy on your dog's waistline. There is a misconception that pork is a fatty meat and isn't good for dogs, yet the facts are highly dependent on the cut of pork and what else you are including in the meal.

Pork chops are packed with flavor for a good reason; they can have over twice the amount of fat as protein, making them a heavy calorie meat similar to 75% lean ground beef.

The Boston butt, or pork shoulder, tips the scales in favor of protein with 1.4 times as much protein as it does fat. This ends up being similar to the 85% lean ground beef.

Boneless pork loin and country-style ribs have 1.6 times as much protein as fat and end up being slightly leaner, but with a good amount of healthy fat. I've selected the country-style ribs because the fat content falls right between that of 85% and 90% lean ground beef with a healthy amount of protein and fat.

For an even leaner meat, pork sirloin tip roast is an option, but I find that you still need to add additional fat in to meet your dog's recommended amount of fat.

PUT PORK IN THE BOWL

The longer the pork is cooked, the tougher it will get, so a light cooking is best to ensure the meat is cooked through but still tender. The pork doesn't have to be browned on the outside as long as it's not bright pink on the inside.

INGREDIENTS

1 pound country-style pork ribs, cut into bite-size chunks (see page xv)
1 clove garlic, minced
¼ teaspoon ground cumin

1. Combine the pork and garlic in a large nonstick skillet over medium heat and then sprinkle the cumin over the meat.

2. Cook for 15 minutes, stirring occasionally.

Yield: 2 cups

KEY NUTRIENTS

Calories 18% • Protein 60% • Total fats 66% • Omega-3 (ALA) 46% • Omega 6 (LA) 39% • Selenium 28% • B_1 (thiamine) 51% • B_3 (niacin) 55% • B_5 (pantothenic acid) 33% • B_6 (pyridoxine) 111%

1 cup of country-style pork ribs has 431 calories; equivalent to about 1¼ cups of commercial dry food.

Replace one-third of your dog's regular meal with the following amount:

10-lb. dog
3 tablespoons

20-lb. dog
¼ cup

40-lb. dog
⅓ cup

60-lb. dog
½ cup

80-lb. dog
⅔ cup

100-lb. dog
¾ cup

PORK & APPLESAUCE

Why do pork and applesauce partner so well together? If you ask me, it's because pork is providing almost 300 percent of your dog's recommended daily allowance of protein, a healthy amount of fat, and many B vitamins. Apples and cinnamon bring a blast of antioxidants and a good amount of fiber to keep the digestive tract healthy.

INGREDIENTS

3 cups cored and diced red apple (from 2 medium-size apples)
⅛ teaspoon ground cinnamon
1 pound country-style pork ribs, cut into bite-size chunks (see page xv)
1 cup chopped green beans
½ cup water

1. Preheat the oven to 400°F.

2. Toss the apple and cinnamon in a casserole dish and then layer with the pork and green beans.

3. Pour the water over the mixture, cover with a lid or foil, and bake for 40 minutes.

Yield: 4 cups

KEY NUTRIENTS

281 calories per cup • Protein 291% •
Carbohydrate-to-protein ratio 0.6 to 1 •
Total fats 314% • Antioxidants 409%

Serve the following amount as a meal, twice a day:

10-lb. dog
⅓ to ¾ cup

20-lb. dog
¾ to 1 cup

40-lb. dog
1⅓ to 2 cups

60-lb. dog
1⅔ to 2½ cups

80-lb. dog
2 to 3¼ cups

100-lb. dog
2⅓ to 3¾ cups

PORK & THREE VEGGIE P'S

Cooking this dish in the oven with a small amount of water allows the vegetables to steam lightly and create a broth to help spread the flavor around. When the bulk of the meal is gone, your dog will be excited to see there is still a little broth left at the bottom of the bowl. Additionally the broth helps to prevent food from sticking to the bottom of the casserole dish—even without added fat.

INGREDIENTS

2½ cups diced potato
¼ teaspoon ground cumin
1 clove garlic, minced
1 pound country-style pork ribs, cut into bite-size chunks (see page xv)
1 cup chopped snow peas
½ cup water
¼ cup chopped parsley

1. Preheat the oven to 400°F.

2. Toss the potato, cumin, and garlic in a casserole dish and then layer with the pork and snow peas.

3. Pour the water over the mixture, cover with a lid or foil, and bake for 40 minutes.

4. Remove from oven and mix the parsley into the pork mixture.

Yield: 5 cups

KEY NUTRIENTS

244 calories per cup • Protein 285% • Carbohydrate-to-protein ratio 0.8 to 1 • Total fats 283% • Antioxidants 152%

Serve the following amount as a meal, twice a day:

10-lb. dog
½ to ¾ cup

20-lb. dog
¾ to 1⅓ cups

40-lb. dog
1½ to 2¼ cups

60-lb. dog
2 to 3 cups

80-lb. dog
2⅓ to 3⅔ cups

100-lb. dog
2¾ to 4⅓ cups

P.O.P.S. (PORK, OATS, PUMPKIN, & SPINACH)

While you're grilling pork ribs for your own dinner, you can put this meal together and let it simmer. By the time your ribs are done, so is this meal for your dog. Then while you are enjoying your barbecue, feed your dog al fresco.

INGREDIENTS

2 cups water
¾ pound country-style pork ribs, cut into bite-size chunks (see page xv)
1 cup whole oats
½ cup frozen spinach, thawed
1 cup canned pure pumpkin

1. Bring the water to a boil in a 2-quart saucepan.

2. Add the pork and lower the heat to medium.

3. Cover the pan with a lid slightly askew and cook for 5 minutes.

4. Stir in the oats and spinach and then lower the heat to low.

5. Allow the oats to simmer for 10 minutes before removing from heat and mixing in the pumpkin.

Yield: 4 cups

KEY NUTRIENTS

301 calories per cup • Protein 262% • Carbohydrate-to-protein ratio 1.1 to 1 • Total fats 259% • Antioxidants 83%

Serve the following amount as a meal, twice a day:

10-lb. dog
⅓ to ⅔ cup

20-lb. dog
¾ to 1 cup

40-lb. dog
1¼ to 1¾ cups

60-lb. dog
1½ to 2⅓ cups

80-lb. dog
2 to 3 cups

100-lb. dog
2¼ to 3½ cups

BACON

What would the world be like if dogs had their say? Instead of a closet of clothes, there would be a closet of tennis balls. There would never be baths; instead, long hikes in a rainy forest would get them clean, all but their muddy feet. Refrigerators would have handles accessible to dogs or—even better—be bark activated. And every food would taste like bacon.

Sunday mornings we make pancakes and bacon and puddles of drool form between the front paws of our dogs. I liberally treat with blueberry pancakes, but hold back on the bacon. Okay, maybe just a small bite. A whole slice of bacon brings 43 calories—equivalent to about 3 tablespoons of commercial dry dog food—and meets 62 percent of a 40-pound dog's sodium intake. With 17 percent fat, it's not a terrible food, but it should be used in moderation.

Of more concern are the nitrates used to produce bacon. To negate the effect of nitrates, the USDA requires bacon to have added antioxidants. Avoiding nitrates altogether is simple; just purchase nitrate-free bacon. It may not be as pink, but it will be just as delicious and good for both you and your dog when given as a treat.

Dogs don't have the same worries about cholesterol as we do, so occasionally (and I mean less than once a month) I replace the tablespoon of fat I'm using to prepare a meal with an equal measure of bacon fat. Although bacon fat doesn't have the same benefits as coconut oil, it's slightly lower in calories and overall fat and high on flavor. That said, dogs with serious illnesses are better off without the added sodium. (Sorry, pups.)

KEY NUTRIENTS

Calories 1% • Total fats 5% • Sodium 18%

Occasional allowance:

10-lb. dog
¹⁄₁₀ **slice**

20-lb. dog
¼ **slice**

40-lb. dog
⅓ **slice**

60-lb. dog
⅓ **slice**

80-lb. dog
½ **slice**

100-lb. dog
⅔ **slice**

BACON POWDER—A LITTLE GOES A LONG WAY

Make more things taste like bacon with an easy-to-create bacon powder. Oats are included to help absorb the scent and flavor and counteract some of the salt and fat.

INGREDIENTS

3 strips bacon
2 tablespoons oats

1. Fry, bake, or microwave the bacon the way you normally would for yourself. Make sure most of the fat is rendered off and the bacon is crispy but not blackened. I prefer doing this in the microwave for 4½ minutes with a paper towel over it, so the stovetop doesn't end up splattered with grease.

2. Set the cooked bacon on a paper towel and blot the excess grease away, until dry.

3. Grind the oats in a blender or clean coffee grinder until a fine powder results.

4. Transfer the oats to a small bowl and similarly grind the bacon.

5. Mix the oats and bacon together and refrigerate in an airtight container.

Yield: 4 tablespoons

KEY NUTRIENTS

301 calories per cup • Protein 262% • Carbohydrate-to-protein ratio 1.1 to 1 • Total fats 259%

Occasional allowance:

10-lb. dog
½ teaspoon

20-lb. dog
¾ teaspoon

40-lb. dog
1 teaspoon

60-lb. dog
1½ teaspoons

80-lb. dog
2 teaspoons

100-lb. dog
2½ teaspoons

CLAMS

Long before you arrive at the beach, the sound of surf and the scent of the sea will notify your dog of the destination. It's a challenge to contain the canine frenzy as you open the car door when you get there, but you manage to grab the leash and escort your dog to the beach. Pulled over the dunes, both you and your dog are relieved to reach the point where the leash is no longer needed. The click of the leash might as well be a gunshot starting a race. Sensing something in the sand, your dog paws at it a bit before moving on and returning to joyful running or chasing a ball. The scent of an almost discovered treasure will stick in his mind, something to dream about when it's time to go home, rest, and nap.

The clam that got away can still make it into the dog bowl and be a savory souvenir of your trip to the beach. The scent will remind your dog of the treasure left behind, while more than a half dozen nutrients work to nourish the brain and contribute to the function of synapses imprinting your dog's memories of the sea.

KEY NUTRIENTS

Calories 7% • Protein 40% • Total fats 5% • Omega-3 (DHA) 38% • Omega-3 (EPA) 25% • Carbohydrates 5 g • Phosphorus 18% • Potassium 24% • Sodium 23% • B_{12} (cyanocobalamin) 88%

1 cup of drained clams has 227 calories; equivalent to about ⅔ cup of commercial dry food.

Add it to the bowl:

10-lb. dog
¼ cup

20-lb. dog
⅓ cup

40-lb. dog
⅔ cup

60-lb. dog
¾ cup

80-lb. dog
1 cup

100-lb. dog
1¼ cups

CLAM BAKE

A typical clambake has a variety of seafood, potatoes, onions, corn on the cob, and sausage. Delicious for us, but a bit much for a dog. Let's simplify it by focusing on the clams and ditching the onions, corn, and sausage your dog doesn't need. To make it even better, this only takes about 40 minutes in the oven and you don't have to dig a pit in the yard. If you already have holes in your yard, maybe somebody was suggesting you make this for dinner.

INGREDIENTS

1 tablespoon coconut or olive oil
1¼ pound red potatoes, diced (about 4 cups)
1 red bell pepper, seeded and chopped
2 (6.5-ounce) cans chopped clams with juice

1. Preheat the oven to 400°F.

2. Grease an 8-inch square baking dish with the oil.

3. Toss the potato and red peppers in the baking dish, then pour over the clams.

4. Cover with a lid or foil, and bake for 40 minutes.

Yield: 4½ cups

KEY NUTRIENTS

214 calories per cup • Protein 285% • Carbohydrate-to-protein ratio 1.5 to 1 • Total fats 126% • Antioxidants 315%

Serve the following amount as a meal, twice a day:

10-lb. dog
⅔ to 1 cups

20-lb. dog
1 to 1½ cups

40-lb. dog
1¾ to 2½ cups

60-lb. dog
2 to 3⅓ cups

80-lb. dog
2¾ to 4 cups

100-lb. dog
3 to 5 cups

CHOW ON THE CLAMS

The first time I made this, the dogs came running as soon as they smelled the first can of clams being opened. Frank, my picky eater, was especially interested in the clams. When it came time to eat, Frank cleaned his bowl obsessively. Clams may not be on the menu every night, but it's a meal Frank certainly loves in rotation, and your dog will as well.

INGREDIENTS

2 (6.5-ounce cans) chopped clams, with juice

2 cups water

1 cup uncooked brown rice

1 red bell pepper, seeded and chopped

1 cup frozen peas

½ cup fresh parsley

1. Combine the clams, water, rice, bell pepper, peas, and parsley in a 2-quart saucepan.

2. Bring the mixture to a boil over high heat.

3. Lower the heat to low and cook for 40 to 50 minutes, stirring occasionally. The rice should absorb almost all the water without sticking to the bottom of the pan.

Yield: 4 cups

KEY NUTRIENTS

290 calories per cup • Protein 171% • Carbohydrate-to-protein ratio 3.2 to 1 • Total fats 120% • Antioxidants 77%

Serve the following amount as a meal, twice a day:

10-lb. dog
⅓ to ⅔ cup

20-lb. dog
¾ to 1¼ cups

40-lb. dog
1⅓ to 1¾ cups

60-lb. dog
1⅔ to 2½ cups

80-lb. dog
2 to 3 cups

100-lb. dog
2⅓ to 3⅔ cups

DRIED FISH

Could there be anything more interesting to your dog than a walk around the neighborhood? The chance to inhale new scents, to make his mark and burn off a little energy has to be one of a dog's favorite activities. Going to the dog park takes it up a notch by adding old and new friends. Or what about a hike? Maybe your dog goes nuts for a few hours investigating a totally wild area, then crashes for hours.

It's always good to take along a training treat, and my latest favorite is dried anchovies. Usually about an inch long and looking like little minnows, they are a low-calorie treat that provides a small omega-3 fatty acid benefit. They're dry and irresistible with a scent to compete against the outside world and return your dog's attention back to you. Most grocery stores don't often carry dried fish, so it may take a bit of research to find them. My favorite source is our local Asian grocery stores. (It's also the place I most easily find gizzards, hearts, and other offal for the dogs.) When you walk in, there are scents you can't identify, fruits you may not have tasted before (dragonfruit is delicious!), and a great source of variety meats. So, this is what it must be like for your dog to go someplace different and interesting.

Purchase fish products without any added MSG (monosodium glutamate) or other preservatives.

FISH SWIMMING IN CIRCLES

I keep a sealed container of Cheerios mixed with dried fish in the laundry room. Whenever I'm folding laundry and want a little company, I give a whistle and the dogs come scrambling down the stairs. They get a few fish-scented treats and a fish or two as a treat for keeping me company. These are also a great training treat.

INGREDIENTS

1 cup plain Cheerios
½ cup dried sardines or anchovies

1. Mix the cereal and fish together, and then seal in an airtight container for up to 2 weeks. Treat liberally!

Yield: 1½ cups

Serving size per day as a treat:

10-lb. dog
1 tablespoon

20-lb. dog
2 tablespoons

40-lb. dog
3 tablespoons

60-lb. dog
¼ cup

80-lb. dog
⅓ cup

100-lb. dog
½ cup

MACKEREL

Greyhounds are known to reach speeds up to 45 miles per hour, making them one of the fastest breeds around. They're perfect for running in a straight line or chasing prey, but as soon as the race is over, the greyhound is ready to take a nap. The Alaskan husky can achieve speeds about half that of the greyhound but can sustain the speed for much longer—all while pulling a sled. Both breeds are remarkable for their achievements, but are hardly interchangeable for the unique requirements needed in each racing environment.

1 cup of canned mackerel has about 300 calories; equivalent to about ¾ cup of commercial dry food.

Omega-3 fatty acids can be sourced from either plants or animals, and like the greyhound and husky, the different sources have different purposes and benefits. Flaxseeds, chia seeds, and pumpkin seeds contain alpha-linolenic acid (ALA), which can contribute to the fight against cancer and enhance brain function; but what your dog's body really runs on is eicosapentaenoic acid (EPA) and docosahexaenoic acid (DHA). Although your dog can convert some of the ALA into EPA and DHA, it's not enough to support the body's entire requirement. Supplying EPA and DHA as part of the diet, by including fish or meat from grass-fed animals, is far better in reducing inflammation and furthering cognitive development. Such foods as mackerel can provide a healthy dose of EPA and DHA when fed as part of your dog's diet two or three times a week.

Replace 10 percent of your dog's regular meal with the following amounts:

10-lb. dog
2 tablespoons

20-lb. dog
3 tablespoons

Whenever possible, purchase mackerel without such additives as sugar and monosodium glutamate, a flavor enhancer that overstimulates neurotransmitters in the brain. Mackerel packed in water or tomato sauce is preferable over mackerel packed in oil, because your dog will already be receiving enough fats in his diet.

40-lb. dog
¼ cup

60-lb. dog
⅓ cup

80-lb. dog
½ cup

KEY NUTRIENTS

Calories 6% • Protein 30% • Total fats 15% • Omega-3 (DHA) 225% •
Omega-3 (EPA) 123% • B_3 (niacin) 46% • B_{12} (cyanocobalamin) 26% • D_3 69%

100-lb. dog
½ cup

MACKEREL MIX-IN—MEAL TOPPER

Mackerel can be used in place of salmon in salmon cakes for your plate, but it's also beneficial for your dog and easy to prepare. With a wide variety of vegetables, fruits, and fish rich in omega-3 fatty acids, this meal topper is a must for any dog. Using canned mackerel and chopping the vegetables in a food processor enhances digestibility without your having to cook anything. Don't worry about those tiny mackerel bones; they're really soft and will break down even further in the food processor.

INGREDIENTS

1 (15.5-ounce) can mackerel
1 garlic clove
1 medium-size carrot
1 medium -size red bell pepper, seeded
½ cup frozen spinach, thawed
1 medium-size red apple, stemmed and cored
½ cup blueberries

1. Drain and rinse the mackerel.

2. Place the mackerel and garlic in a food processor and process until chopped finely.

3. Roughly chop the vegetables and apple, then add to the food processor.

4. Add the blueberries and pulse five or six times to chop all vegetables finely.

Yield: 5½ cups

KEY NUTRIENTS

133 calories per cup • Protein 427% • Carbohydrate-to-protein ratio 0.4 to 1 • Total fats 209% • Antioxidants 380%

Serve the following amount once per day, replacing one-fifth of your dog's normal meal.

10-lb. dog
1 to 3 tablespoons

20-lb. dog
¼ cup

40-lb. dog
⅓ cup

60-lb. dog
⅓ to ½ cup

80-lb. dog
⅓ to ¾ cup

100-lb. dog
½ to ¾ cup

SARDINES

I purchase about 30 cans of sardines a year—some find their way to a sardine salad (like tuna, but even better for you) or on slices of toasted baguette. However, most of the sardines are bound for the dog bowl. About the same price as a can of tuna fish, sardines are higher in the omega-3 fatty acids your dog needs and many are packed in tomato sauce, which is a nice lycopene bonus for your pet. The lycopene acts as an antioxidant and fights against multiple types of cancer. Lycopene is best absorbed when eaten with a little fat, which the sardines are providing along with protein.

When I go downstairs to get sardines, the dogs follow me and watch me intently. When I grab the can, Flynn does a couple of quick circles, then dashes back up the stairs and into the kitchen before I even have my foot on the first stair. He'll sit politely until he sees the can opener and then starts weaving in and out of my legs like a cat. I don't blame the sardines for his feline behavior because he acts the same way when there's cheese or vegetables on the counter. Since Flynn is part basenji and has been known to vocalize in amazing ways, I have promised him if he ever "meows," I'll give him a can of sardines all to himself. So far he hasn't succeeded, but he's trying.

KEY NUTRIENTS

Calories 11% • Protein 42% • Total fats 35% • Omega-3 (DHA) 189% • Omega-3 (EPA) 176% • Omega 6 (LA) 55% • B_3 (niacin) 51% • B_{12} (cyanocobalamin) 43% • D 60%

1 (3.5-ounce) can of sardines has approximately 170 calories; equivalent to about ½ cup of commercial dry food.

Add it to the bowl:

10-lb. dog
⅕ can

20-lb. dog
⅓ can

40-lb. dog
½ can

60-lb. dog
⅔ can

80-lb. dog
1 can

100-lb. dog
1¼ cans

SARDINES & VEGETABLES— MEAL TOPPER/WEIGHT LOSS

Just because your dog has to lose a little weight doesn't mean he has to go around with a rumbling stomach. With a mere 80 calories per cup, this meal topper can be used to liven up mealtime or help your pet lose weight. By switching out an equal measure of commercial food, this fishy treat reduces the number of calories in your dog's meal by approximately 18 percent. On the plus side, your pup will be receiving essential omega-3 fatty acids and quality protein.

INGREDIENTS

1 (3.5-ounce) can sardines
1 cup chopped carrot
1 cup chopped zucchini

1. Combine all ingredients in a small bowl with a fork until the sardines are broken up and well distributed throughout the mixture.

Yield: 3 cups

KEY NUTRIENTS

80 calories per cup • Protein 13% • Carbohydrate-to-protein ratio 0.7 to 1 • Total fats 11% • Antioxidants 5%

To achieve weight loss, replace 25 percent of your dog's normal diet with an equal measure of this recipe. For other dogs, replace 10 percent of the normal diet with the following amount:

10-lb. dog
¼ cup

20-lb. dog
⅓ cup

40-lb. dog
½ to ¾ cup

60-lb. dog
⅔ to 1 cup

80-lb. dog
¾ to 1 cup

100-lb. dog
¾ to 1⅓ cups

SALMON

Plenty of commercial pet foods contain salmon, a fish both high in protein and healthy fats. However, if you've ever had overcooked salmon, you know how a poor preparation can ruin a perfectly good meal. Now imagine the salmon is dried at high temperatures and has the texture of particleboard. Not so appetizing, even when intended for the dog bowl.

Salmon (and trout) needs to be cooked for dogs to prevent infestation by parasites, the cause of salmon poisoning in dogs. A light cooking will kill the parasites but retain the delicate flavor and texture. Unfortunately, another danger with fish is the buildup of toxic chemicals in the skin and internal organs, particularly an issue with farmed salmon. It's recommended to purchase wild salmon and to discard the fish skin for both people and pets.

Salmon is very high in vitamin D, which is essential for bone health and the health of the immune system. The omega-3 fatty acids and selenium reduce inflammation, fight cancer, protect against heart disease, and maintain healthy mental functions, so it's worth keeping fish in the diet. To detox the body when feeding fish, include chlorophyll-filled vegetables, such as green beans, broccoli, kale, and parsley.

The bones in canned fish are quite soft and should be digestible by most dogs. If you find any pieces that cause concern, just mash it with a fork rather than try to debone it, to retain the calcium.

KEY NUTRIENTS

Calories 5% • Protein 29% • Total fats 11% • Omega-3 (DHA) 201% •
Omega-3 (EPA) 90% • B$_3$ (niacin) 53% • B$_{12}$ (cyanocobalamin) 17% • D$_3$ 131%

1 cup of salmon has 248 calories; equivalent to about ¾ cup of commercial dry food.

Replace 10 percent of your dog's regular meal with the following amounts:

10-lb. dog
2 tablespoons

20-lb. dog
3 tablespoons

40-lb. dog
¼ cup

60-lb. dog
⅓ cup

80-lb. dog
½ cup

100-lb. dog
½ cup

SALMON SAUCE

Is your dog fishing for something new in the bowl? Not only will this provide a fantastic fish flavor, it's going to provide the omega-3 fatty acids to lower inflammation and build a healthy brain.

INGREDIENTS

1 cup chopped carrot
2 cups chicken stock
1 cup chopped green beans
1 (7.5-ounce) can pink salmon

1. Combine the carrot and chicken stock in a 2-quart saucepan. Bring to a boil, then lower the heat to low and simmer for 15 minutes.

2. When the carrot has cooled down, combine with the green beans and salmon in a blender and purée until smooth. The salmon sauce can be stored for up to 4 days in the fridge. Freeze in ice cube trays for easy serving and then transfer to an airtight container. Store frozen cubes for up to 2 months.

Yield: 5 cups

KEY NUTRIENTS

135 calories per cup • Protein 16% • Carbohydrate-to-protein ratio 0.4 to 1 • Total fats 7% • Antioxidants 11%

Add it to the bowl:

10-lb. dog
1 tablespoon

20-lb. dog
2 tablespoons

40-lb. dog
3 tablespoons

60-lb. dog
¼ cup

80-lb. dog
⅓ cup

100-lb. dog
½ cup

SALMON & VEG

All of the fish recipes in this book can be great meal toppers to commercial foods because they provide a huge boost of protein, omega-3 fatty acids, and vitamin D. If you would like to use this as a meal topper, replace one-third of your dog's regular meal with an equal portion of the Salmon & Veg. Despite the amount of healthy fats included, this meal ends up being very low in calories and high in protein.

INGREDIENTS

1 tablespoon coconut or olive oil
3 cups chopped summer squash
1 cup chopped carrot
1 garlic clove, minced
½ cup frozen spinach, thawed
2 (15-ounce) cans pink salmon, drained

1. Heat the oil in a large skillet over medium heat.

2. Add the squash, carrot, and garlic and cook for 30 minutes, stirring occasionally.

3. Mix in the spinach and cook for another 5 minutes.

4. Remove from the heat and stir in the salmon.

Yield: 6 cups

KEY NUTRIENTS

190 calories per cup • Protein 468% • Carbohydrate-to-protein ratio 0.2 to 1 • Total fats 261% • Antioxidants 88%

Serve the following amount as a meal, twice a day:

10-lb. dog
⅔ to 1 cup

20-lb. dog
1 to 1¾ cups

40-lb. dog
2 to 2¾ cups

60-lb. dog
2⅓ to 3¾ cups

80-lb. dog
3 to 4¾ cups

100-lb. dog
3⅔ to 5½ cups

SALMON HASH

When you open a can of salmon, curious noses lead to wagging tails. Try it and see. First open a can for yourself and make some delicious salmon patties. If that doesn't bring your dog around, open a second can and show your dog what he has been missing, with this tasty dish.

INGREDIENTS

2 tablespoons coconut or olive oil
1½ pounds diced potato, cleaned of green spots and eyes
¾ cup water
½ teaspoon ground fennel
1 cup chopped Swiss chard
1 (15-ounce) can pink salmon, drained

1. Preheat the oven to 400°F. If using coconut oil, place the oil in a large baking dish and put the dish in the oven while you're preparing the potatoes. Otherwise, grease the dish with the olive oil.

2. Add the potatoes and water to the dish.

3. Sprinkle the fennel over the potatoes, cover with a lid or foil, and bake for 30 minutes.

4. Add the Swiss chard, re-cover the dish, and bake for another 10 minutes.

5. Mix in the salmon.

Yield: 5 cups

KEY NUTRIENTS

231 calories per cup • Protein 260% • Carbohydrate-to-protein ratio 1.3 to 1 • Total fats 241% • Antioxidants 273%

Serve the following amount as a meal, twice a day:

10-lb. dog
½ to ¾ cup

20-lb. dog
1 to 1⅓ cups

40-lb. dog
1⅔ to 2⅓ cups

60-lb. dog
2 to 3 cups

80-lb. dog
2½ to 3¾ cups

100-lb. dog
3 to 4½ cups

SALMON & RICE

The great thing about rice is how it soaks up flavor. And this dish has a lot of flavor to soak up. If you'd like to use this for a meal topper for commercial food, use two cans of pink salmon; the protein will increase by 50 percent and the carbohydrate-to-protein ratio will be one to one. As a meal topper, replace up to half of your dog's regular meal with an equal amount of Salmon & Rice.

INGREDIENTS

3½ cups water
1 cup uncooked brown rice
1 cup chopped sugar snap or snow peas
1 cup chopped Brussels sprouts
1 (15-ounce) can pink salmon, drained

1. Bring the water to a boil over high heat in a 2-quart saucepan.

2. Add the rice and allow the pan to return to a boil, then lower the heat to low.

3. Cover the pan with a lid and cook the rice for 40 minutes.

4. Stir in the vegetables and cook for 5 more minutes. All the liquid should be absorbed and the vegetables softened.

5. Remove from the heat and stir in the salmon.

Yield: 5 cups

KEY NUTRIENTS

244 calories per cup • Protein 267% • Carbohydrate-to-protein ratio 1.7 to 1 • Total fats 112%

Serve the following amount as a meal, twice a day:

10-lb. dog
½ to ¾ cup

20-lb. dog
¾ to 1⅓ cups

40-lb. dog
1½ to 2¼ cups

60-lb. dog
2 to 3 cups

80-lb. dog
2⅓ to 3⅔ cups

100-lb. dog
2¾ to 4⅓ cups

TUNA

While accessible and inexpensive, tuna isn't my favorite fish for dogs. I'd rather use mackerel and salmon in the dogs' meals and sardines as a supplemental food because they have more calcium, zinc, omega-3 fatty acids, and vitamin D. What tuna does have going for it is more selenium and protein, plus it's an overall leaner fish if your dog needs to trim down. Many pantries are stocked with tuna, so it's a good and convenient addition to brighten up the dog bowl.

Buy tuna packed in water rather than oil and, of course, look for sustainably harvested tuna.

KEY NUTRIENTS

Calories 6% • Protein 34% • Total fats 8% • Omega-3 (DHA) 199% • Omega-3 (EPA) 74% • Sodium 68% • Selenium 26% • B$_3$ (niacin) 48% • D$_3$ 21%

1 cup of tuna has 272 calories; equivalent to about ¾ cup of commercial dry food.

Add it to the bowl:

10-lb. dog
2 tablespoons

20-lb. dog
3 tablespoons

40-lb. dog
3 tablespoons

60-lb. dog
⅓ cup

80-lb. dog
⅓ cup

100-lb. dog
⅓ cup

TUNA COOKIES

Cookies don't need gluten to taste good—not if they have tuna in them. This cookie is super simple and contains oats instead of wheat flour. If your dog is sensitive to gluten, be sure to buy oats certified to be gluten free.

INGREDIENTS

1 teaspoon coconut or olive oil (optional)
2 cups oats
1 large egg
1 (5-ounce) can tuna fish packed in water, drained
¼ cup fresh parsley

1. Preheat the oven to 400°F. Lightly grease a cookie sheet or line it with a silicone mat.

2. Pulse the oats in a food processor for 1 minute. The oats should have a fine, flourlike texture.

3. Stir all the ingredients together in a medium-size bowl.

4. Drop a tablespoon of cookie dough onto the prepared baking sheet. Flatten the cookie to about ¼-inch thickness and repeat with the remaining dough.

5. Bake for 10 minutes.

6. Store the cookies in the refrigerator in an airtight container for up to 1 week or in the freezer for up to a month.

Yield: 18 cookies

Daily allowance:

10-lb. dog
1 cookie

20-lb. dog
1 cookie

40-lb. dog
2 cookies

60-lb. dog
2 cookies

80-lb. dog
3 cookies

100-lb. dog
3 cookies

CHAPTER 2

VARIETY WITH VEGETABLES

The main purpose of including produce in your dog's diet is to provide your pet with something not found in commercial foods: a wide variety of antioxidants. Fruits and vegetables are loaded with antioxidants beyond those the manufacturer has to add simply because they are also required vitamins and minerals. Except for corn and peas used to boost protein levels and the increasingly ubiquitous sweet potatoes, there are few fruits and vegetables in most commercial foods. Out of 78 commercial foods I surveyed that contained apples, none of them had a significant amount of apple in them and 85 percent had more salt than they did apples. If you're buying a product with blueberries on the ingredient panel, you're receiving far less than you'd think—probably only one or two blueberries per bag.

As part of natural chemical processes, molecules throughout your dog's body lose an electron and become unstable, earning the name *free radicals* as they go about destroying cell membranes and DNA with the same intensity as your dog trying to retrieve a ball from underneath the couch. Antioxidants provide a generous supply of electrons and distract the free radicals away from causing damage; much like your dog forgetting the ball when you open the refrigerator.

Antioxidants are attracted to different types of cells in the body, so a variety is needed to ensure you're protecting your dog from nose to tail. Phytochemicals that create the taste, scent, color, texture, and shapes of fruits and vegetables have antioxidant behavior in the body. Antioxidants don't stop at mellowing free radicals; the same antioxidants continue protecting your dog against many other diseases. There are thousands of phytochemicals, not just the half-dozen found in commercial foods.

Some of the new heroes in your dog's bowl:

- *Apigenin*: Parsley and other greenish-yellow vegetables provide a potent fighter against prostate cancer, bladder cancer, and leukemia.

- *Chlorogenic acid*: Tomatoes, pears, apples, and potatoes have antioxidant, antimicrobial, anti-inflammatory, and colon and liver cancer-fighting benefits due to this phytochemical.

- *Chrysin*: A contribution from honey protects against illness by combatting bacteria, aflatoxins, and salmonella.

- *Cyanidin*: The pigment that gives plums, apples, berries, and red cabbage their reddish-purple hue reduces arthritis pain, battles mycotoxins, preserves DNA integrity, and lowers the risk of kidney stones.

ORGANIC OR NOT?
It's not just what the food doesn't contain; also, in many cases how it is grown can make food more nutritious. Think about how an organic farmers need to maintain healthy soil. Rather than adding synthetic fertilizers, they often add compost and other natural materials that break down into the soil and are then absorbed by the plants to increase the amount of nutrients.

❧ *Delphinidin, malvidin, and petunidin*: A brotherhood of blue pigments found in blueberries, plums, and even ripe bananas fights gum infections and cancer and may help protect against UV damage.

❧ *Epicatechin*: Apples, apricots, pears, and cherries provide this powerful antioxidant along with insulin-resistance lowering, glucose tolerance, and cancer-fighting and anti-inflammatory properties.

❧ *Fisetin*: Apples are the best source for dogs to receive this protector of neural pathways and stimulator of growth in nerve cells.

❧ *Isorhamnetin*: Green leafy vegetables and asparagus hammer against free radicals, inflammation, bacteria, and cancer.

❧ *Kaempferol*: Kale, spinach, chard, and broccoli contain one of the strongest antioxidants for protection against allergies, bacteria, cancers, diabetes, inflammation, and viruses.

❧ *Luteolin*: Just about every vegetable and many fruits contain this phytochemical that's anti-everything: anti-inflammatory, antitumor, antileukemic, anticataract, anticancer, antibacterial, antiangiogenic, and antioxidant.

❧ *Myricetin*: Rutabaga, berries, cranberries, and cabbage might be novel food items for your dog, but they bring along a phytochemical with a host of benefits to protect

DOG VEG

When I'm cooking and have a small amount of vegetable scraps, I toss them right into the dog bowl. If there's more than a cup of vegetables, I chop them up and store in my freezer's "Dog Veg" container and use it when making stock or substituting in meals. Beyond vegetables, I also add extra grated ginger, parsley, and herbs. The Dog Veg container contains a lot of variety and keeps the dog bowl interesting.

against neurological decline, cancer, candidiasis, bacteria, inflammation, and peri-odontal disease.

🐾 *Pelargonidin*: The orange pigment in berries and kidney beans protects the brain, reduces the risk for colon and liver cancer, and assists diabetics with insulin sensitivity.

🐾 *Peonidin*: A red pigment found in fruits also protects against cancer and mental decline.

🐾 *Quercetin*: Such greens as kale, apples, garlic, berries, and even buckwheat contain this potent antioxidant that provides every property mentioned in discussion of all these other antioxidants.

🐾 *Rutin*: Best found in buckwheat, asparagus, cranberries, and the skin of apples, this antioxidant pairs well with pineapple to help alleviate pain and intensifies the benefits of vitamin C. On its own, rutin protects the brain, skin, eyes, and blood sugar levels.

Your doctor would tell you to eat more fruits and vegetables for all these same benefits and more. It's time to load up the produce bin. Throughout the following pages, you'll find surprising ways to incorporate fruits and vegetables into meals for your dinner plate and the dog bowl.

ASPARAGUS

Spring is a time to celebrate, and what vegetable heralds the arrival of spring more than asparagus? Maybe the reason why asparagus grows so tall and straight is that it's trying to pack so many phytochemicals inside. There are saponins that reduce blood cholesterol and inflammation; quercetin that protect your dog from allergies and cancer; kaempferol, with antibacterial, antiviral, and antioxidant benefits; rutin, with anticancer, anti-inflammatory, antioxidant, and cognition-protective properties; and rutin's buddy, glutathione, which helps detoxify the body, break down carcinogens, and prevent the development of cataracts. Asparagus has more glutathione than any other vegetable.

The soluble fiber inulin, which enables asparagus's stature, also acts as a prebiotic, feeding beneficial bacteria in the gut and inhibiting the growth of pathogenic bacteria. And then there is the similarly named amino acid asparagine, which acts as a natural diuretic and is essential to cognitive function.

Asparagus contain a lower amount of pesticide residues, so conventionally farmed produce may be acceptable.

On Your Plate

- For a delicious salad dressing, combine 1 cup of steamed asparagus, 1 teaspoon each of lemon juice and Dijon mustard, ¼ cup of olive oil, ¼ teaspoon of salt, and a couple of grinds of fresh pepper in a food processor. Blend until smooth.

In the Dog Bowl

- The tougher, lower portion of asparagus contains the highest levels of rutin, so don't toss them in the compost bin; finely chop, then steam or roast them at 425°F for 15 minutes.

- Asparagus tips can be fed raw.

SHARDS OF SPEARS

Asparagus should be cooked until very tender and/or chopped finely to help your dog digest it well. Let's do both.

INGREDIENTS

10 spears asparagus or a mixture of spears and stems
½ cup water or chicken stock

1. Split each asparagus stem lengthwise, then chop into fine pieces. Or use a food processor to chop by pulsing 15 times.

2. Bring the water to a boil over high heat in a small saucepan.

3. Add the asparagus, cover, and lower the heat to low.

4. Simmer for 15 minutes, or until the asparagus is very soft and the liquid has evaporated.

Yield: ⅔ cup

KEY NUTRIENTS

Calories 1% • Protein 3% • Total fats 0% • Carbohydrates 2 g • Potassium 6% • Iron 9% • A 20% • B$_9$ (folate) 25% • K 88% • Antioxidants 16%

1 spear of asparagus has a mere 3 calories; equivalent to about less than a teaspoon of commercial dry food.

Add it to the bowl:

10-lb. dog
2 tablespoons

20-lb. dog
3 tablespoons

40-lb. dog
3 tablespoons

60-lb. dog
⅓ cup

80-lb. dog
⅓ cup

100-lb. dog
⅓ cup

BROCCOLI

If vegetables had their own motto, broccoli's would be "less is best." Like many vegetables, broccoli is often overcooked, inspiring a lifetime aversion for many people—and it might as well do so, because when broccoli is overcooked, many of the nutrients end up in the water along with most of the flavor. When you steam broccoli for just 5 minutes, it's tender but not mushy and remains a vibrant green, leaving even asparagus envious. Best of all the sulfur compounds in broccoli remain in the vegetable rather than the cooking water. The sulforaphane in broccoli detoxifies and protects the body from cancer by removing potential carcinogens from the body. Broccoli also provides additional support in the fight against various cancers along with antibacterial, antiviral, and antioxidant benefits.

Conventionally grown broccoli has a high amount of pesticide residue; buying organic is recommended. Look for firm florets with either a dark green, purple, or bluish hue to select a product higher in beta-carotene, vitamin C, and sulforaphane.

Thanks to this vegetable being so nutrient dense with only 34 calories per cup, you and I are encouraged to eat at least 2 cups of broccoli per week. For dogs, however, the "less is best" motto still holds. Broccoli at higher doses can lead to stomach upset in some dogs. To reap the benefits of broccoli, feed it in rotation with other vegetables. It doesn't have to just be the crown, either; broccoli stalks can be shared with your dog, whole or finely diced and lightly steamed. Let your dog choose.

On Your Plate

- Add the small, delicate leaves from broccoli stems to your salads.

- Sprouted broccoli contains almost the same amount of glucosinolates as mature broccoli, so if you're not a fan of cooked broccoli, try adding the sprouts to salads or sandwiches.

- Roast broccoli with a little olive oil, minced garlic, salt, and pepper at 450°F for 20 minutes.

In the Dog Bowl

- The peelings of broccoli stems can be incorporated raw into your dog's meal. If you don't eat the stems, just keep peeling the stems until they're gone: You've just made broccoli noodles!

- Roasted broccoli is a treat that can be shared with dogs as well.

KEY NUTRIENTS

Calories less than 1% · Protein 1% · Total fats 0% · Carbohydrates 2 g · B$_9$ (folate) 11% · K 77% · Antioxidants 4%

1 cup of broccoli has 34 calories; equivalent to about 3 tablespoons of commercial dry food.

Add it to the bowl:

10-lb. dog
1 tablespoon

20-lb. dog
2 tablespoons

40-lb. dog
3 tablespoons

60-lb. dog
⅓ cup

80-lb. dog
½ cup

100-lb. dog
⅔ cup

BUTTERNUT SQUASH

I've had a love-hate relationship with butternut squash for years. It's packed with a diverse amount of vitamins and minerals, fiber, and carotenoids that protect the health of the heart and eyes. It is one of my favorite squashes for both the nutrition and the diverse ways it can be used. However, the process of peeling a butternut squash always seemed worse than peeling a whole bag of potatoes. And then I decided the most difficult part would just go to the dogs, peel and all. Yep, the skin is edible for both man and beast.

Winter squash, such as pumpkin, is ranked low for pesticide residues; however, when feeding the skin to your dog, be sure to buy organic.

For an easy way to cut a butternut squash, use a heavy, sharp knife. I use my cleaver. Cut off the stem, and then cut off the bulbous part. Set the seed-filled portion aside. Then stand the relatively straight part on its end and carefully slice off the skin, rotating around the cylinder of squash in about eight turns. You'll lose a little of the squash flesh with this process but it definitely pays off with the time and effort saved. From here you can slice, cube, or shred it and use it in your favorite recipe. The bulb end and scraps can be shared with your dog.

On Your Plate

- Roast or steam butternut squash, then give it a good mashing. Use the mashed squash to replace one-third of the cheese in your macaroni and cheese recipe; it will add the color and creaminess people are expecting without the added fat.

- Toss with two cloves of chopped garlic, some olive oil, and ground cumin, and roast at 425°F for 25 minutes, or until soft. Combine with black beans and avocado for a tortilla filling or enjoy it all on its own.

In the Dog Bowl

- Thinly sliced butternut squash can be quickly cooked in a non-stick frying pan over medium heat for 6 to 8 minutes.

- Use chunks of butternut squash as a stopper for your pet's Kong.

- Butternut squash cut into sticks can be shared raw with your dog. Use the amounts listed in the following recipe as a serving guideline.

BUTTER' IN THE BOWL

With hardly any effort, you can roast the extra bits of butternut squash or other squashes and provide your dog with a healthy dose of fiber and beta-carotene to protect against diabetes, cancer, and heart disease.

1. Preheat the oven to 425°F.

2. Scoop the seeds out of the bulb end and cut into eight to ten wedges.

3. Chop the wedges and skin into bite-size bits, then spread in a lightly oiled baking dish.

4. Bake for 25 minutes.

KEY NUTRIENTS

Calories 4% • Protein 3% • Total fats 1% • Carbohydrates 16 g • Magnesium 16% • Potassium 24% • A 607% • B_3 (niacin) 20% • B_6 (pyridoxine) 30% • B_9 (folate) 29% • E 14% • Antioxidants 6%

1 cup of butternut squash has 63 calories; equivalent to about 3 tablespoons of commercial dry food.

Add it to the bowl:

10-lb. dog
¼ cup, diced

20-lb. dog
⅓ cup, diced

40-lb. dog
⅔ cup, diced

60-lb. dog
¾ cup, diced

80-lb. dog
1 cup, diced

100-lb. dog
1¼ cups, diced

CABBAGE (AND BRUSSELS SPROUTS)

It would be a shame if Labrador retrievers only came in one color. From the palest of yellow to a slightly more orange appearance (however, still called yellow) to light and dark chocolate and the deepest black, one of the world's favorite dog breeds exemplifies the qualities we love about dogs; good natured, playful, loyal, and loving. Color doesn't affect their temperament, behavior, or athletic ability; it's just an aesthetic left behind on your pants after you pet them.

In the vegetable world, it's a little different. Color greatly influences the nutritional effect of foods due to the different phytochemicals producing a plant's color. While all cabbages can provide detoxifying and cancer-fighting glucosinolates, red cabbage sets itself apart from its green brothers of the field because of its unique color. Cyanidin, the same chemical providing give blackberries their color and their antitoxin effect, is greater in a serving of cabbage than in a serving of blackberries. In green cabbages, the amount of folate is two to four times higher than in the red variety. If you're looking for a heavyweight fighter against cancer, look to savoy cabbage, which is higher in cancer-fighting chemicals. Brussels sprouts when steamed are particularly effective in lowering cholesterol and are higher in gluconisolates than any of its brothers from the cabbage family. In most other respects, all cabbages are very similar nutritionally, so rather than forsake one for the other, try rotating them through your diet and your dog's.

Cabbage contains a lower amount of pesticide residues. Conventionally farmed and organic produce can both be good choices.

1 cup of raw, shredded cabbage has 17 calories; equivalent to about 1 tablespoon of commercial dry food.

Add it to the bowl:

10-lb. dog
1 tablespoon

20-lb. dog
2 tablespoons

40-lb. dog
¼ cup

60-lb. dog
¼ cup

80-lb. dog
⅓ cup

100-lb. dog
½ cup

On Your Plate

- Thinly slice ½ pound of Brussels sprouts and sauté over medium heat with 3 tablespoons of butter (or bacon fat) until soft. Add some salt and pepper, then top with a poached or fried egg for your weekend breakfast.

In the Dog Bowl

- Try raw shredded cabbage right in the bowl. Some dogs love the crunch.

- Roast Brussels sprouts tossed in olive oil for 30 minutes at 350°F. Share a couple with your dog, then add a little salt and pepper for yourself.

KEY NUTRIENTS

Calories 0% • Protein 1% • Total fats 0% • Carbohydrates 1 g • B$_9$ (folate) 7% • C 8 mg • K 58% • Antioxidants 6%

SAUTÉED CABBAGE

Lightly sautéing shredded cabbage or Brussels sprouts with vinegar helps soften the vegetables and provides a little tang of flavor many dogs enjoy.

INGREDIENTS

2 cups shredded cabbage or Brussels sprouts
2 tablespoons apple cider vinegar

1. Place the cabbage in a nonstick skillet and sprinkle with the vinegar.

2. Cook over medium heat for 12 to 15 minutes, until the cabbage is wilted.

Yield: 1 cup

KEY NUTRIENTS

Calories 0% • Protein 1% • Total fats 0% • Carbohydrates 1 g • B_9 (folate) 7% • C 8 mg • K 58% • Antioxidants 6%

Add it to the bowl:

10-lb. dog
1 tablespoon

20-lb. dog
2 tablespoons

40-lb. dog
¼ cup

60-lb. dog
¼ cup

80-lb. dog
⅓ cup

100-lb. dog
½ cup

WHAT'S BUBBLING?

After you've made coleslaw for a barbecue, don't throw away the extra cabbage—ferment it instead. Fermenting vegetables increases digestibility and provides enzymes and probiotics beneficial to the bacteria in the gut. Making fermented vegetables for yourself retains the benefits removed when commercial products are pasteurized. Including beets in this recipe also provides antioxidants as well as anti-inflammatory and detoxification support. If you have a food processor, use it to chop the beets, and then chop the cabbage. The smaller bits will start creating juices sooner. Otherwise, grate or slice the beets and cabbage.

INGREDIENTS

2 cups grated or julienned beets
4 cups finely chopped cabbage
2 teaspoon salt (sea salt works best)
2 teaspoons olive oil

1. Toss the beets, cabbage, and salt in a large bowl, mixing them thoroughly.

2. Pack the vegetable mixture into a clean quart-size jar and crush with a wooden spoon so the vegetables release their juices. Let sit for 2 to 3 hours, then crush with the spoon again until the vegetables are completely covered in liquid. Scrape down the sides of the jar and ensure there are no pockets of air in the mixture and that a thin layer of water covers the surface.

3. Pour the olive oil on top of the vegetables and cover with a lid. Set the jar in a cool, dry place for 3 to 5 days. The longer the vegetables sit, the more lactic acid and beneficial bacteria are produced, so you can let the vegetables ferment for up to 3 weeks. The vegetables should be tangy and slightly softened when ready.

4. After you open the jar, store it in the refrigerator for up to 3 weeks.

Serving size per day:

10-lb. dog
1½ teaspoons

20-lb. dog
2 teaspoons

40-lb. dog
1 tablespoon

60-lb. dog
1½ tablespoons

80-lb. dog
2 tablespoons

100-lb. dog
3 tablespoons

5. The vegetables should be served along with some of
    the juices.

Yield: 3 cups

KEY NUTRIENTS

4 calories per tablespoon • Protein 1% • Carbohydrate-to-protein ratio 5 to 1 •
Total fats 0% • Antioxidants 7%

CARROTS

The ability of dogs to read our body language and facial expressions is unparalleled in the animal world. We require education to understand the canine body language and to know a tail wag can indicate aggression or simply confidence depending on the position, speed of the wag, and other body signals.

Dogs are naturals at reading body language from one another and us because they are adept at picking up visual clues and aligning their understanding within their social structures. The eyes are the window to a dog's soul, but windows work two ways and dogs definitely use their eyes to take in the outside world as well.

With only one-eighth of the optic nerves that we have, dog don't see the same definition of colors that we do, but they make up for it in low-light conditions and being able to see 240 degrees in their field of vision in comparison to our 180 degrees. Although your dog may not be able to see the precise color of a carrot, the color of the carrot is exactly what enables your dog to see. Vitamin A acts as a potent antioxidant and protects the health of the eyes as well as the immune system.

When you hold a carrot up for your dog and she sits to wait for the treat, your pet knows that correct behavior is part of your social contract. Carrots and other foods high in carotenoids end up being both the reward and the facilitator between the two of you.

Carrots contain a high amount of pesticide residues; purchasing organic carrots is recommended.

1 cup of sliced carrot has 52 calories; equivalent to about less than ¼ cup of commercial dry food.

Add it to the bowl:

10-lb. dog
2 tablespoons

20-lb. dog
3 tablespoons

40-lb. dog
¼ cup

60-lb. dog
⅓ cup

80-lb. dog
½ cup

100-lb. dog
⅔ cup

KEY NUTRIENTS

Calories 2% • Protein 1% • Total fats 1% • Carbohydrates 6 g • A 430% • B_6 (pyridoxine) 12% • Antioxidants 5%

On Your Plate

- From Diane Morgan's *Roots* cookbook I learned carrot greens are also edible and can be made into a pesto. I've adapted the idea using what I had in the kitchen to pretty fantastic results on top of pasta, to top winter soups or a grilled steak. Combine 2 cups of washed carrot greens, ¼ cup of pistachios or cashews, 1 garlic clove, ⅓ cup of olive oil, and ¼ cup of extra-virgin olive oil in a food processor and pulse 12 to 15 times, or until reduced to a fine mixture. Add salt and pepper to your taste.

In the Dog Bowl

- If you're buying organic carrots, give them a quick wash under the water and then peel the carrots directly into the dog bowl to make "dog spaghetti."

- After stuffing your dog's Kong, up the level of difficulty by corking it with a carrot. Cut the carrot flush with the Kong's opening and it will drive your dog crazy.

CAULIFLOWER

"No thanks," some dogs will say when you offer them a tennis ball. While others go crazy for the fuzzy yellow sphere, it fails to excite more than a sniff in others. "How about a squeaky ball?" you ask. "Nope, not my thing," they reply, turning away from the sight of it. "How about a Frisbee?" You can almost hear a click in the dogs' neck as they turn to you, "What?" From that moment on the Frisbee never fails to excite. That's kind of how I feel about cauliflower.

Raw, steamed, and boiled cauliflower has always been something on my plate with little interest. Then we started roasting cauliflower and it's a completely different vegetable. When it is caramelized and slightly nutty tasting, I actually look forward to cauliflower being on the plate. We're eating much cauliflower now and so are the dogs.

To say cauliflower pales in comparison to its cruciferous brethren (broccoli, Brussels sprouts, and cabbage) isn't just a reference to color. In some respects cauliflower is nutritionally a few steps behind, but it's very low in calories and carbohydrates and is less likely to cause stomach upset than broccoli, resulting in the offering of a slightly larger portion size. Vitamins and phytochemicals provide detoxification, antioxidants, and cancer-fighting benefits, while a good dose of fiber keeps the digestive system running smoothly.

Cauliflower has a lower amount of pesticide residues. Both conventionally grown and organic can be good choices.

On Your Plate

- When you're tired of kale and don't feel like another spinach salad, try a different type of greens: cauliflower greens. Treat them as you would if you're sautéing any other green with some olive oil, garlic, salt, and pepper. They're also great combined in scrambled eggs with a little sharp Cheddar cheese.

In the Dog Bowl

- Don't toss cauliflower stems in the compost—throw them in the dog bowl. Just finely chop and mix them into your dog's meal or sauté for 5 minutes in a little olive oil over medium heat.

- 1 cup of raw cauliflower has 25 calories; equivalent to about 2 tablespoons of commercial dry food.

GOLDEN CAULIFLOWER

Sharing cauliflower with your dog can be as simple as chop and serve; however, both you and your dog could use a daily dose of turmeric. While cauliflower is not a nutritional superstar, it makes for a low-carb and tasty vehicle for the most powerful antioxidant-laden food in your kitchen.

INGREDIENTS

1 head cauliflower (about 5 cups after chopping)
3 tablespoons coconut or olive oil
3 cloves garlic, minced
1 tablespoon ground turmeric
1 teaspoon salt

1. Preheat the oven to 400°F.

2. Remove the stem from the cauliflower and chop the florets into 1-inch pieces.

3. Toss the cauliflower with the remaining ingredients on a rimmed baking sheet and bake for 30 minutes. The cauliflower should be lightly browned and tender.

Yield: 4 cups

KEY NUTRIENTS

Calories 2% • Protein 4% • Total fats 1% • Carbohydrates 5 g • Potassium 14% • B_5 (pantothenic acid) 9% • B_6 (pyridoxine) 25% • B_9 (folate) 43% • K 51% • Antioxidants 9%

Add it to the bowl:

10-lb. dog
3 tablespoons

20-lb. dog
⅓ cup

40-lb. dog
½ cup

60-lb. dog
⅔ cup

80-lb. dog
1 cup

100-lb. dog
1¼ cups

GREEN BEANS

Your dog's body doesn't just produce tons of hair to shed all over the couch and your freshly ironed clothes. The canine digestive system also produces two vitamins to meet their daily requirements our human body cannot: vitamins C and K.

Vitamin C (ascorbic acid) is produced internally from glucose and plays an important role in the production of collagen, the healing of wounds and for its antioxidant activity. Vitamin C enhances the body's absorption of iron, other minerals, and vitamins; reduces the risk of cataracts; and supports the immune system. Supplementing vitamin C is especially useful for dogs fighting cancer.

We can produce 50 percent of the vitamin K we require, whereas dogs can usually produce enough to meet their full requirement. Vitamin K helps produce prothrombin, a protein necessary for blood clotting and helps in the formation of bones by promoting the joining of calcium molecules to create the structure of bone. Antibiotics do a number on the beneficial bacteria responsible for producing vitamin K; supplementing a diet with vegetables is especially recommended for dogs finishing an antibiotic regimen or those recovering from diarrhea.

Plenty of leafy green vegetables contain vitamins C and K, as do green beans. A serving of green beans will provide your dog with 94 percent of the RDA of vitamin K, supplementing what's already being manufactured. Green beans supply silicon, important for the formation of connective tissues, a host of antioxidants, and starches that act like fiber to help regulate blood glucose levels in diabetics.

Green beans retain a high amount of pesticide residues. Buying organic is highly recommended.

1 cup of green beans has 48 calories; equivalent to about 3 tablespoons of commercial dry food.

Add it to the bowl:

10-lb. dog
2 tablespoons

20-lb. dog
3 tablespoons

40-lb. dog
¼ cup

60-lb. dog
⅓ cup

80-lb. dog
½ cup

100-lb. dog
⅔ cup

On Your Plate

- During the summer, I carefully tend our tarragon plants and put this forgotten herb to use with chicken or as a chopped herb over quickly sautéed green beans. Combine with a splash of balsamic vinegar over the beans, a little salt and pepper, and you've got a side dish that will have people asking, "What's in these beans?" (Dogs are not fans of tarragon.)

In the Dog Bowl

- Green beans are a healthy treat for all dogs, but particularly for those with diabetes. Feed the beans fresh or even frozen by themselves or chopped up as an additive to your dog's meal.

KEY NUTRIENTS

Calories 2% • Protein 2% • Total fats 0% • Carbohydrates 5 g • Manganese 10% • A 14% • B_9 (folate) 7% • C 8 mg • K 94% • Antioxidants 17%

GREEN BEANS & BACON

My family's favorite side dish was created by my grandmother: fresh green beans, onion, vinegar, and bacon fat topped with salt and pepper. Onion, of course, should not be fed to dogs, but I can't resist sharing fresh green beans with a little bacon flavor.

INGREDIENTS

1 teaspoon bacon grease
1 cup chopped green beans

1. Heat the bacon grease in a skillet over medium heat.

2. Add the green beans and cook for 8 to 10 minutes, or until softened.

Yield: 1 cup

KEY NUTRIENTS

84 calories per cup • Protein 5% • Carbohydrate-to-protein ratio 4 to 1 • Total fats 17% • Antioxidants 25%

JICAMA

Every once in a while you'll see a dog defying classification. While many of the lovable dogs are mutts, and I use the term lovingly because we've had quite a few, some are actually very rare breeds with a pedigree linking them to very specific purposes. The Hungarian Pumi is a terrier bred to catch rats, but looks more intended to be huggable. The word has it the Pumi is also a pretty good dancer. The Kai Ken is the most ancient breed of dog in Japan and was bred to hunt boar and is even able to climb trees. The most unique hairstyle might belong to the Bergamasco shepherd dog, which has three types of hair forming woolly dreadlocks. Bred for sheep herding, it's an extremely loyal and intelligent dog.

As vegetables go, jicama, too, has not been fully discovered. The appearance doesn't have much to suggest giving it a try; the inedible, scarred flesh is tough and requires a bit of peeling to find the slightly sweet-tasting flesh. With a crunchiness a little bit like an apple and a bit like water chestnuts, it's a great snacking food. Nutritionally it doesn't offer much to make it a standout food. What it does offer is a good source of inulin, the

1 cup of jicama has 49 calories; equivalent to about 3 tablespoons of commercial dry food.

Add it to the bowl:

10-lb. dog
2 tablespoons

20-lb. dog
3 tablespoons

40-lb. dog
⅓ cup

60-lb. dog
½ cup

80-lb. dog
½ cup

100-lb. dog
⅔ cup

soluble fiber food for beneficial bacteria in the digestive system. In addition, inulin helps the body to absorb calcium from other foods to create strong bones. Low in carbohydrates and calories, jicama is also a good alternative for people wanting to avoid giving potatoes to their dogs yet still provide a good source of fiber to balance out the digestive system.

On Your Plate

- Jicama Fries: Peel a jicama, then slice into ¼-inch-square strips. Toss with a tablespoon of olive oil, your favorite spices, and ½ teaspoon of salt, then bake for 45 minutes at 400°F.

- Fruit Salads: Add some julienned jicama to your fruit salads for an extra crunch.

In the Dog Bowl

- Both the jicama fries and extra julienned (or grated) jicama can be incorporated directly into your dog's meal.

- When pairing jicama dishes with a grilled hamburger for yourself, combine equal amounts of ground beef and grated jicama into a grilled patty for your dog.

KEY NUTRIENTS

Calories 2% • Protein 1% • Total fats 0% • Carbohydrates 6 g • Potassium 5% • B_9 (folate) 6% • C 13 mg

KALE

It wasn't long ago kale was just a decorative garnish inside the meat case at the local butcher. Then all of a sudden it was on every restaurant menu and appearing on every nutritional blog. There was curly kale, red kale, purple kale, and dinosaur kale (a.k.a. lacinato, but it's much easier to get kids to eat it if you call it dinosaur kale.) While not always popular with diners because of its slightly bitter, pungent flavor, kale is extremely popular inside the body.

In addition to a very healthy dose of vitamin K (eight times as much as green beans) kale is exploding with phytochemicals that benefit both people and canines. No other food contains as much per canine serving of lutein and zeaxanthin for healthy eyes and the prevention of cataracts. Again kale wins first place in providing your dog with the most kaempferol per serving to fight against bacteria, viruses, oxidation, and inflammation due to allergies, diabetes, and cancer. Just when you are tired of watching kale take the podium, it makes a last appearance to take the trophy for providing the best source of isorhamnetin, which also has antioxidant and inflammatory properties. As if the trophy shelf wasn't full enough, kale also receives honorable mention for its copper, quercetin, folate, vitamin A, and vitamin C content. Whether your dog is striving for the tennis ball trophy or that of the most lovable dog, pairing your pet with kale will make them a formidable team.

Collard greens and kale have a high amount of pesticide residue—buying organic is highly recommended.

1 cup of kale has 33 calories; equivalent to about 2 teaspoons of commercial dry food.

Add it to the bowl:

10-lb. dog
2 tablespoons

20-lb. dog
3 tablespoons

40-lb. dog
⅓ cup

60-lb. dog
½ cup

80-lb. dog
½ cup

100-lb. dog
⅔ cup

KEY NUTRIENTS

Calories 1% • Protein 3% • Total fats 1% • Carbohydrates 3 g • Copper 17% • A 136% • B$_9$ (folate) 36% • C 40 mg • K 798% • Antioxidants 6%

"DIRTY" KALE CHIPS/KALE DUST

Kale chips were supposed to be the new potato chip, but it didn't get very far. Although a much healthier alternative than potatoes, they have an airy bite to them. Dirty them up and they'll be more appetizing for both you and your dog and still offer health benefits for both of you. Prepackaged kale makes this recipe even easier.

INGREDIENTS

½ **pound kale**
1 **tablespoon melted coconut oil or olive oil**
3 **cloves garlic, minced**
2 **teaspoons nutritional yeast**
3 **tablespoons freshly grated Parmesan cheese**
⅛ **teaspoon salt**

1. Preheat the oven to 350°F.

2. Clean the kale and dry well in a salad spinner or by tying the leaves up in a clean kitchen towel and gently rubbing.

3. Cut out the stems by folding the leaf in half and cutting along the stem at a slight angle from the thinnest tip to the thickest end. Set the stems aside and use in any recipe calling for leafy green vegetables.

4. Combine the oil, garlic, nutritional yeast, and cheese in a large bowl. Add the kale and toss well to coat.

5. Spread out the kale on a baking sheet and bake for 10 to 12 minutes.

6. Set aside a portion for your dog, then add the salt to your own.

Yield: 3 cups

KEY NUTRIENTS

103 calories per cup • Protein 9% • Carbohydrate-to-protein ratio 1.4 to 1 • Total fats 20% • Antioxidants 28%

Add it to the bowl:

10-lb. dog
3 tablespoons

20-lb. dog
¼ cup

40-lb. dog
⅓ cup

60-lb. dog
½ cup

80-lb. dog
¾ cup

100-lb. dog
1 cup

Have a little extra? Rub it in your hands to turn it into kale dust to top your dog's food.

NORI (DRIED SEAWEED)

Nori is a type of seaweed, which itself is a member of the algae family, dried and used to wrap sushi or, increasingly, as a snack. Although feeding raw fish is out of the question for dogs (due to the risk of parasites), you can still provide a taste of the sea with different types of seaweed. You can feed a square inch or two to your dog, but it's best to think of seaweed as a flavor enhancer and as a seasoning rather than a food to feed by itself.

All the minerals found in the sea are also found in nori, making it one of the widest sources of minerals available, including many microminerals, such as boron (important for bone development), chromium (a contributor to controlling blood sugar levels), and molybdenum (an aid to liver detoxification and fat metabolism). The minerals are all in small amounts, so they just give a little nutritional push, especially since the serving size will be so small.

Other types of seaweed that can be used are wakame, kombu, dulse, and kelp, all with similar attributes. The main difference in the varieties of dried seaweed is their iodine levels. Dulse has about 4 times as much iodine as nori, wakame has about 5 times as much, while kombu has almost 70 times as much in an equal measure. Dogs with thyroid issues should not be fed seaweed unless approved by your veterinarian.

Nori is increasingly available in grocery stores and a wide variety of seaweeds is often available at Asian grocery stores.

On Your Plate

- Toast 1 crumbled sheet of nori, ½ cup of sesame seeds, 1 teaspoon of red pepper flakes, and ½ teaspoon of salt in a skillet over medium-low heat for 3 to 4 minutes. Grind in a blender or food processor until powdered and then use as a seasoning for meats, rice, salads, or over vegetables.

In the Dog Bowl

- Crumble nori sheets and mix into your dog's food

- Add 1 teaspoon of crumbled nori to any meal recipe or when making stock for your dog.

KEY NUTRIENTS

Calories 0% • Protein 0% • Total fats 0% • Carbohydrates 0.1 g • Iodine 14%

1 teaspoon of dried nori has 1 calorie; equivalent to less than one morsel of commercial dry food.

Add it to the bowl:

10-lb. dog
¼ teaspoon

20-lb. dog
⅓ teaspoon

40-lb. dog
⅔ teaspoon

60-lb. dog
¾ teaspoon

80-lb. dog
1 teaspoon

100-lb. dog
1¼ teaspoons

PARSNIPS, RUTABAGAS, & TURNIPS

Farmers rotate their crops to prevent the spread of disease and control pest populations. We could all use a little more crop rotation through our vegetable bins to help prevent disease in us and our canine pals as well. We tend to eat more potatoes than any other vegetable, and your dog may already have potatoes in her commercial dog food. Luckily, more root vegetables are waiting for their turn on your plate than in the dog bowl and they bring some great benefits.

Parsnips are often referred to as carrots that have seen a ghost. With a slightly sweet, slightly bitter flavor, parsnips are a great roasting vegetable. Although they lack pigmentation and therefore many phytochemicals, one potent phytochemical in parsnips (falcarinol) has antifungal, antibacterial, and cancer-fighting properties.

The yellow and purple flesh of the rutabaga already points out there are some helpful antioxidants inside. Rutabagas provide more of the phytochemicals myricetin and apignen per serving than any other vegetable, both of which are shown to have anticancer, anti-inflammatory, and neuroprotective benefits.

No other food will provide your dog as much of the glucosinolates per serving as turnips will. Glucosinolates bring the pungent, mustardy hint of flavor to turnips along with cancer-fighting power and the ability to partner with folate, vitamin C, and other phytochemicals to purge free radicals and toxins from the body. And it doesn't stop there; turnip tops are even higher in minerals, vitamins, and phytochemicals to boost the body even more. Including these greens in modest amounts add up to big gains.

All three root vegetables are lower in calories than potatoes (turnips have about one-third the calories), and provide significant amounts of fiber, B vitamins, and in rutabagas and turnips, a high amount of omega-3 fatty acids. Maybe it's time to rotate some of these root vegetables into your diet and your dog's.

1 cup of parsnip has 100 calories; equivalent to about ⅓ cup of commercial dry food.

1 cup of rutabaga has 49 calories; equivalent to about 3 tablespoons of commercial dry food.

1 cup of turnip has 36 calories; equivalent to about 2 tablespoons of commercial dry food.

On Your Plate

- Use half of any of these root vegetables and half potatoes when making mashed potatoes, for an even healthier side dish.

In the Dog Bowl

- Incorporate peelings of parsnips, rutabagas, and turnips into the pot when making stock for your dog.

ROOT FOR THE VEGETABLES

You can cook one of these vegetables or a combination of them fairly quickly. If using more than one, extend the cooking time to the longest time necessary.

INGREDIENTS

⅔ **pound parsnips, rutabagas, or turnips**
¼ **cup water**

1. Preheat the oven to 450°F.

2. Peel the parsnips or rutabagas. Turnips can just be washed briefly.

3. Cut into 1-inch chunks and then transfer to a baking dish. Add the water to help steam them and prevent sticking.

4. Roast the parsnips for 20 minutes; the rutabagas for 35 minutes; and the turnips for 30 minutes.

5. The vegetables should be tender. If roasting a combination of vegetables, roast for the longest length of time one of them requires.

Yield: 2 cups

KEY NUTRIENTS OF PARSNIPS

Calories 6% • Protein 3% • Total fats 1% • Magnesium 13% • Potassium 24% • Manganese 31% • B_6 (pyridoxine) 17% • B_9 (folate) 68% • K 101%

KEY NUTRIENTS OF RUTABAGAS

Calories 3% • Protein 3% • Omega-3 (ALA) 34% • Carbohydrates 11 g • Fiber 17% • Magnesium 9% • Potassium 20% • B_6 (pyridoxine) 18% • B_9 (folate) 21%

KEY NUTRIENTS OF TURNIPS

Calories 2% • Protein 2% • Total fats 0% • Omega-3 (ALA) 25% • Carbohydrates 8 g • Fiber 13% • B_6 (pyridoxine) 16% • B_9 (folate) 15%

Add it to the bowl:

10-lb. dog
¼ **cup**

20-lb. dog
⅓ **cup**

40-lb. dog
⅔ **cup**

60-lb. dog
¾ **cup**

80-lb. dog
1 cup

100-lb. dog
1¼ cup

PEAS

I'm pretty grateful dogs can't write letters; otherwise, there would have been an avalanche of correspondence from dogs refusing to eat their peas. It's quite amazing how even when they're hidden inside a meal, dogs can lick each pea clean and leave a pile of them in the bowl. At the same time we're seeing an increase in the number of pet foods utilizing pea flour because of the protein content.

If your dog is a fan of fresh peas, by all means, include them. Mashing the peas makes them more palatable because it breaks down the skin many dogs are reluctant to bite into. Serving them frozen can also be a healthy snack. Split peas are more likely to be well received than fresh peas because they lack the dreaded skin. When using split peas in recipes, they provide a good balance of carbohydrates to protein (2 to 1) and have 9 of the 10 proteins your dog needs in good amounts. Plus, they offer a healthy amount of fiber to support the digestive system.

Peas are low in calories but provide 13 percent of your dog's necessary fiber per serving, along with folate to support healthy DNA, iron for immune system, and supply of oxygen to cells; vitamin C to support what your dog is already producing; and manganese for the formation of bones, tissues, cartilage, and proteins.

1 cup of frozen or raw peas has 111 calories; equivalent to about ⅓ cup of commercial dry food.

Add it to the bowl:

10-lb. dog
¼ cup

20-lb. dog
⅓ cup

40-lb. dog
⅔ cup

60-lb. dog
¾ cup

80-lb. dog
1 cup

100-lb. dog
1¼ cup

KEY NUTRIENTS

Calories 7% • Protein 15% •
Total fats 2% •
Carbohydrates 20 g •
Manganese 20% •
A 120% • B$_1$ (thiamine) 34% •
B$_3$ (niacin) 29% •
B$_9$ (folate) 58% • K 136%

PEPPERS

When I want to read a something to make me laugh and maybe tear up a bit at the end, I'll often reach for a story about a dog. One of my favorite books to date was *The Art of Racing in the Rain* by Garth Stein. I couldn't turn a page without one emotion or another requiring me to have some sort of mini-outburst, whether it was a chuckle or frown. At one point our hero, the dog Enzo, has a run in with a jar of pickled jalapeños. Enzo puts his digestive distress to good use, but has to live through the experience. I don't think Enzo will be trying jalapeño peppers again.

A jalapeño pepper is just not a good idea for dogs. A whole jar is even worse. Switch it to sweet instead of spicy and we're on to something. Make sure you're not pushing off green bell peppers and are using sweet red, yellow, or orange bell peppers, and you've got a crunchy, sweet, and juicy snack for your canine's canines to chew on.

Peppers are rich in a variety of carotenoid nutrients, often containing up to 30 different phytochemicals in one pepper. The carotenoids support the health of your dog's vision as well as providing antioxidant activity and sulfur compounds to fight cancer.

Conventionally grown peppers contain a high amount of pesticide residues. Buying organic is highly recommended.

KEY NUTRIENTS

Calories 0% • Protein 0% • Total fats 0% • Carbohydrates 1 g • A 29% • B_6 (pyridoxine) 9%

1 cup of diced red bell pepper has 29 calories; equivalent to about 2 tablespoons of commercial dry food.

Add it to the bowl:

10-lb. dog
1 tablespoon

20-lb. dog
2 tablespoons

40-lb. dog
3 tablespoons

60-lb. dog
¼ cup

80-lb. dog
¼ cup

100-lb. dog
⅓ cup

POTATOES

The most fashionable vegetable in your dog's food might just be potatoes. A fashion or trend first shows up unexpectedly, slowly catches on before becoming mainstream, then shortly afterward falls from grace after the uniqueness and original idea is diluted. A few years ago, potatoes showed up to replace corn in dog food, particular along with duck as part of an allergy diet. Soon potatoes became the "it" replacement for grains and today the trend has reached the point where the quality of a whole potato has been diminished into potato protein, potato fiber, and potato starch ingredients. The whole potato is better nutritionally, with skin containing more than 25 percent the vegetable's nutrients. Potatoes are a source of carbohydrates for energy, contain only a third of the calories in an equal amount of dog food, and are your dog's highest source of caffeic acid, an antioxidant with antineurodegenerative and anti-inflammation effects.

White potatoes are great when mashed, but there are so many more varieties out there. Waxy potatoes have a lower glycemic index, while red, gold, and purple potatoes bring an even higher antioxidant kick due to the phytochemicals creating their colorful hues.

The only color not good for dogs is green. Any green spots or green tones to the flesh should be discarded along with any eyes. These green spots contain solanine, which can be toxic to both you and your dog. Because potatoes rank highly on foods with pesticide residue, spend a few extra bucks for your potatoes and buy something colorful and organic.

Lightly steam potatoes for 30 minutes or bake for 400°F for 30 minutes, covered.

KEY NUTRIENTS

Calories 7% • Protein 6% • Total fats 1% • Carbohydrates 26 • Potassium 31% • B$_3$ (niacin) 19% • B$_6$ (pyridoxine) 61% • B$_9$ (folate) 18% • C 30 mg • Antioxidants 78%

1 cup of potato has 115 calories; equivalent to about ⅓ cup of commercial dry food.

Add it to the bowl:

10-lb. dog
¼ cup

20-lb. dog
⅓ cup

40-lb. dog
⅔ cup

60-lb. dog
¾ cup

80-lb. dog
1 cup

100-lb. dog
1¼ cups

THANKFUL FOR MASHED POTATOES

The day before our Thanksgiving company arrives, I make this to keep the dogs busy and away from the appetizer platter. Stuffing this in a Kong provides dogs a taste from the dinner table while also providing leftovers for the next couple of days while you are enjoying your own leftovers. Why the parsley? To prevent someone from eating the wrong leftovers.

INGREDIENTS

½ pound potatoes, cleaned and cubed into 1-inch cubes (3 cups)
4 cups water
1 turkey liver
1 turkey gizzard
1 turkey heart
¼ cup fresh parsley

1. Discard the turkey neck from the giblet pack if it was included.

2. Combine the potatoes, water, and turkey giblets in a 2-quart saucepan and bring to a boil over medium-high heat. Cook for 20 minutes, just until the potatoes are easily pierced with a fork.

3. Drain the potatoes and giblets, reserving the stock for any recipe requiring homemade stock.

4. Remove three-quarters of the turkey liver and set it aside for use in other recipes.

5. Chop the remaining one-quarter of the turkey liver and the gizzard, heart, and parsley until finely minced.

6. Combine the turkey, parsley and potatoes in a medium-size bowl and mash with a potato masher or spoon. (Don't worry; dogs don't care about a few lumps.)

Yield: 3 cups

Add it to the bowl:

10-lb. dog
¼ cup

20-lb. dog
⅓ cup

40-lb. dog
⅔ cup

60-lb. dog
¾ cup

80-lb. dog
1 cup

100-lb. dog
1¼ cups

KEY NUTRIENTS

172 calories per cup • Calories 11% • Protein 27% • Carbohydrate-to-protein ratio 2 to 1 • Total fats 10%

PUMPKIN

The best time of the year to stock your dog's medicine cabinet is in November. That's when I buy a case of canned pumpkin because it's on sale for a fraction of the price you'll find it at other times of the year. I call pumpkin "the Great Equalizer" because the blend of soluble and insoluble fiber helps bring dogs who are suffering from either diarrhea or constipation back to center. The sizable scoop you add contains only 25 percent of the calories in an equal measure of commercial food. However, pumpkin is not a junk food; it also packs in a surprising amount of vitamins and minerals. It's not just medicine for an upset stomach; pumpkin is a food to nourish and protect the whole body.

Fresh or canned pumpkin is a good alternative for making treats for dogs with sensitive stomachs and adding to meals where you might want to tone down the calories and fat content without leaving your pup feeling hungry.

Winter squash, like pumpkin, is ranked low for pesticide residues; when feeding the skin to your dog, buy organic. Be sure to buy *pure* pumpkin—what is marketed as "pumpkin pie filling" contains mace and nutmeg, both of which are toxic to dogs.

KEY NUTRIENTS

Calories 3% • Protein 3% • Total fats 1% • Carbohydrates 10 g • A 129% •
B₉ (folate) 11% • K 66% • Antioxidants 14%

1 cup of canned pure pumpkin has 83 calories; equivalent to about ¼ cup of commercial dry food.

Add it to the bowl:

10-lb. dog
3 tablespoons

20-lb. dog
¼ cup

40-lb. dog
⅓ cup

60-lb. dog
½ cup

80-lb. dog
⅔ cup

100-lb. dog
¾ cup

ALL THE GUTS AND ALL THE GLORY (PUMPKIN)

This pumpkin flour can be sprinkled directly on your dog's food for an added dose of magnesium, potassium, and zinc or used to replace up to one-quarter of the flour in homemade dog cookies.

INGREDIENTS

8 cups pumpkin flesh, seeds, and strings

1. Preheat the oven to 350°F. Line a rimmed baking dish with a silicone mat or parchment paper.

2. Cut any pumpkin flesh into ¼-inch-thick slices and spread the flesh, pumpkin seeds, and strings in a single layer on the baking sheet.

3. Bake for 30 minutes, stir, and then bake for another 30 minutes, or until dried and crispy.

4. Remove the dried pumpkin from the oven and allow it to cool.

5. Use a blender or food processor to grind to a fine powder.

Yield: 2 cups

KEY NUTRIENTS

626 calories per cup •
Protein 4% •
Carbohydrate-to-protein
ratio 3 to 1 • Total fats 6% •
Antioxidants 2%

Add it to the bowl:

10-lb. dog
½ teaspoon

20-lb. dog
1 teaspoon

40-lb. dog
1½ teaspoons

60-lb. dog
2½ teaspoons

80-lb. dog
1 tablespoon

100-lb. dog
4 teaspoons

SNAP AND SNOW PEAS

Take an ingredient like peas and add back the firm bite and crunch provided by the pod, and suddenly dogs think it's the greatest vegetable around. Do they love the sweetness? Or is it the juicy green vegetable reminds them of grass? The reasons for you to provide these pods to your dog might just out weigh your pet's reasons to eat them.

Despite their sweet flavor, snow and snap peas can help manage blood sugar with their dietary fiber and resistant starch, most of which is provided by the pod. Saponins are chemicals that create a foaming action and in many plants different varieties can be toxic to dogs. The saponins in peas are safe for dogs and provide anti-inflammatory and antioxidant benefits. The vitamin C provided is one of the highest amounts your dog will receive per serving, along with lutein and zeaxanthin to protect the eyes and vitamin K for a healthy immune system.

Snow peas contain a high amount of pesticide residues. Buying organic is highly recommended.

NOT SO SNAPPY PEAS

Chomping on either type of peas as a treat is great, but to really ensure your dog receives the most from the nutrients, chop them up and steam lightly to enhance digestibility and absorption.

INGREDIENTS

1 cup snow or snap peas

1. Bring 2 cups of water to a boil in a saucepan fitted with a steamer.

2. Chop the pods into ¼-inch bits and place in the steamer.

3. Cover with a lid and steam for 10 minutes, or until the pods have softened slightly.

KEY NUTRIENTS

Calories 2% • Protein 4% • Total fats 1% • Carbohydrates 5 g • B_6 (pyridoxine) 16% • B_9 (folate) 23% • C 43 mg • K 61%

1 cup of snow or snap peas has 60 calories; equivalent to about 3 tablespoons of commercial dry food.

Add it to the bowl:

10-lb. dog
3 tablespoons

20-lb. dog
3 tablespoons

40-lb. dog
⅓ cup

60-lb. dog
½ cup

80-lb. dog
½ cup

100-lb. dog
⅔ cup

SPINACH

Your dog needs a lot of calcium for healthy formation of bone and to support the cardiovascular, nervous, and muscular systems. A 40-pound dog requires 1,000 mg of calcium per day, the same as you and me. The concern with spinach and other leafy greens has been that their high oxalic acid content robs the body of calcium. The problem with this theory is the oxalic acid only prevents the calcium in the spinach from being absorbed. It doesn't continue preventing the body from absorbing all the other calcium from the diet. And, in fact, about 12 percent of the calcium in spinach remains available. Spinach is a bad place to look for fulfilling your dog's requirement anyway because a reasonable size serving only offers 5 percent of your dog's calcium RDA.

What spinach does offer are a dozen different antioxidants that fight inflammation and cancer, chlorophyll that detoxifies the body, and a huge helping of vitamin K that helps build bone. The only dogs who should not be eating leafy greens are those prone to forming calcium oxalate stones.

Because conventionally grown spinach has a high amount of pesticide residue, I recommend using frozen organic spinach. One cup of frozen spinach is equal to about 12 cups of fresh spinach and it requires minimal preparation because the act of freezing helps to break down the plant's cell structure.

1 cup of frozen spinach has 9 calories; equivalent to about just a few pieces of commercial dry food.

Add it to the bowl:

10-lb. dog
2 tablespoons

20-lb. dog
3 tablespoons

40-lb. dog
⅓ cup

60-lb. dog
½ cup

80-lb. dog
½ cup

100-lb. dog
⅔ cup

KEY NUTRIENTS

Calories 0% • Protein 1% • Total fats 0% • Carbohydrates 0.63 g • Calcium 5% • A 12% • B_9 (folate) 17% • K 189% • Antioxidants 6%

SWEET POTATOES & YAMS

Have you ever been asked if your dog was a certain breed, when he is actually something else? Sometimes the comparisons are amusing and at other times confounding. Owners of a greyhound or whippet can easily distinguish between the two breeds, but some admirers unfamiliar with the breeds just can't get it. The same goes for the loving companions of Norwich, Norfolk, and Cairn terriers. While many breeds may share similar appearance traits, a closer look will reveal their unique differences.

In the United States we often mix up the names of sweet potatoes and yams. The red Garnet yam you buy in the grocery store—turns out it's actually a sweet potato. To distinguish the Garnets from their cousins with the lighter-colored flesh, we started calling them yams. The real yam is a completely different vegetable not often found in most grocery stores, and is usually longer and more cylindrical with a rough, scaly texture.

Despite their name, sweet potatoes actually have a moderate effect on blood sugar levels because of the high amount of accompanying fiber; benefiting diabetics by managing glucose and improving insulin sensitivity. Whether you call it sweet potato or a yam, the more colorful it is, the more antioxidants it contains with purple-fleshed sweet potatoes containing higher amounts of peonidin and cyanidin that protect the digestive system.

Sweet potatoes also contain sporamins, unique proteins that help repair damage to the plant. Inside the body they offer additional antioxidant protection to rival the antioxidants produced within the body.

Conventionally grown sweet potatoes and yams have a fair amount of pesticide residue; buying organic is recommended.

BAKED SWEET POTATOES

This delicious treat also goes great in a Kong once cooled, or up the difficulty level by freezing the Kong overnight.

INGREDIENTS

½ pound sweet potato or yam
Pinch of ground cinnamon
¼ cup water

1. Preheat the oven to 400°F.

2. Cut the sweet potato into ½-inch dice (you should have about 2 cups).

3. Combine the sweet potato and cinnamon in a medium-size casserole dish and then pour in the water.

4. Cover with a lid or foil and bake for 30 minutes, or until the sweet potato is very soft.

Yield: 1½ cups

KEY NUTRIENTS

Calories 4% • Protein 2% • Total fats 0% • Carbohydrates 13 g • Potassium 11% • A 64% • B$_6$ (pyridoxine) 19% • Antioxidants 14%

1 cup of sweet potato has 114 calories; equivalent to about ⅓ cup of commercial dry food.

Add it to the bowl:

10-lb. dog
3 tablespoons

20-lb. dog
3 tablespoons

40-lb. dog
⅓ cup

60-lb. dog
½ cup

80-lb. dog
½ cup

100-lb. dog
⅔ cup

SWEET! POTATO CHIPS!

The first time I made these Sweet! Potato Chips! the dogs went nuts. Since they are done in a skillet, there is no need for added salt or oil. The thinner you cut these the better; you almost want them paper thin. By peeling them lengthwise, you get larger chips for larger dogs.

INGREDIENTS

½ large Garnet yam (¼ pound)

1. Create thin slices by peeling with a potato peeler or slice using a mandoline at the thinnest setting.

2. Heat a nonstick skillet over medium heat. Spread a single layer of sweet potato slices in the pan and allow to cook for 5 minutes, or until the edges are slightly browned and they start to curl. Then turn them over and cook for another 2 minutes, or until the chips have lost most of their moisture and are crispy.

Yield: 1 cup

KEY NUTRIENTS

Calories 4% • Protein 2% • Total fats 0% • Carbohydrates 13 g • Potassium 11% • A 64% • B_6 (pyridoxine) 19% • Antioxidants 14%

10-lb. dog
3 tablespoons

20-lb. dog
3 tablespoons

40-lb. dog
⅓ cup

60-lb. dog
½ cup

80-lb. dog
½ cup

100-lb. dog
⅔ cup

OVEN SWEET POTATO CHIPS

Roasting sweet potatoes results in a slightly thicker slice in the oven, increasing the chewiness and providing a little bit of a crunch around the edges. Since these are low-calorie, feel free to give your dog a generous serving.

INGREDIENTS
1 large Garnet yam (about 1 pound)

1. Preheat the oven to 350°F.

2. Rinse the yam, cut it into ¼-inch-thick slices, and arrange on a baking sheet.

3. Bake the yam for 30 minutes, then flip the slices over. Bake for an additional 15 to 20 minutes, or until dry and chewy. Watch them carefully because the chips start to brown fast.

4. Store extra chips in an airtight container in the refrigerator for up to 5 days.

Yield: 4 cups

KEY NUTRIENTS

Calories 4% • Protein 2% • Total fats 0% • Carbohydrates 13 g •
Potassium 11% • A 64% • B_6 (pyridoxine) 19% • Antioxidants 14%

10-lb. dog
3 tablespoons

20-lb. dog
3 tablespoons

40-lb. dog
⅓ cup

60-lb. dog
½ cup

80-lb. dog
½ cup

100-lb. dog
⅔ cup

ZUCCHINI AND SUMMER SQUASHES

If you grow your own zucchini, you know how one little seed can provide an abundant crop. If you turn your back, the next day you have a baseball bat–size vegetable and you end up trying to share the bounty with anybody you can find. So, why not share with your dog?

Summer squash are 95 percent water with a high vitamin and mineral concentration. At the peak of summer when you have more than enough zucchini, the water content and potassium will help to keep your dog hydrated, while the vitamin B_6 will convert fat into energy to keep your pet zipping around the yard.

"GREATED" ZUCCHINI

If your dog is going to eat his veggies, the least we can do is make it a little more interesting. With a mere teaspoon of bacon grease, we can turn the garden's overflow into something great.

INGREDIENTS

1 teaspoon bacon grease
2 cups grated zucchini

1. Heat a nonstick skillet over medium heat and add the bacon grease. After the grease has melted, pick up the skillet and give it a couple of twists to spread the grease around.

2. Add the zucchini and cook for 8 minutes, or until the zucchini is soft.

Yield: 1 cup

KEY NUTRIENTS

Calories 1% • Protein 3% • Omega-3 (ALA) 37% • Carbohydrates 4 g •
Potassium 16% • Manganese 9% • B_6 (pyridoxine) 28% • B_9 (folate) 23% • K 18%

1 cup of zucchini has 21 calories; equivalent to about 2 tablespoons of commercial dry food. This version adds a few more calories, but your dog will think it's worth it.

Add it to the bowl:

10-lb. dog
¼ cup

20-lb. dog
⅓ cup

40-lb. dog
½ cup

60-lb. dog
⅔ cup

80-lb. dog
¾ cup

100-lb. dog
1 cup

SWEET ZUC' BISCUITS

After summer is over, you'll have to start buying zucchini again because you dog will want more of these delicious cookies. That's okay; they're easy to make.

INGREDIENTS

1 tablespoon coconut or olive oil, plus more for baking sheet (optional)
2 cups oats
2 large eggs
1 tablespoon honey
¼ teaspoon ground cinnamon
2 cups shredded zucchini

1. Preheat the oven to 400°F. Lightly grease a baking sheet with oil, or line with a silicone mat.

2. Pulse the oats in a food processor for 1 minute, until a slightly grainy powder develops.

3. Mix together the eggs, oil, honey, and cinnamon in a medium-size bowl.

4. Stir in the zucchini and then stir in the oats.

5. Drop tablespoonfuls, spaced one inch apart, onto the prepared baking sheet and press slightly to flatten.

6. Bake the biscuits for 25 minutes, or until lightly browned.

7. Store the biscuits in the refrigerator in an airtight container for up to 1 week or in the freezer for up to a month.

Yield: 36 biscuits

KEY NUTRIENTS

87 calories per cup • Protein 15% • Carbohydrate-to-protein ratio 3 to 1 • Total fats 38%

Daily allowance:

10-lb. dog
½ biscuit

20-lb. dog
1 biscuit

40-lb. dog
1 biscuit

60-lb. dog
2 biscuits

80-lb. dog
2 biscuits

100-lb. dog
3 biscuits

CHAPTER 3

FORTIFIED BY FRUIT

Green vegetables can be a difficult sell to dogs, but fruit brings something that dogs enjoy—sweetness. The one thing that does intimidate some dogs, though, is the thin skin of fruits. Simply slicing, chopping, mashing, or puréeing whole fruit can eliminate the resistance of the skin while still ensuring the antioxidants inside and usually closest to the skin have the opportunity to do their magic in your dog's body.

APPLES

Will an apple a day keep the vet away? Let's not put all the pressure on just one fruit or vegetable, since it's much better to provide a wide variety of antioxidants and phytochemicals from a variety of sources. However, many of the nutrients in apples can certainly make a significant contribution toward keeping your pet healthy.

Apples contain insoluble and soluble fibers to aid digestion by keeping things moving along but not too fast. The insoluble fiber prevents constipation while also helping to balance the pH of the intestines, preventing microbes in the digestive system from producing cancerous precursors. Soluble fiber, pectin in particular, partners with the antioxidants in apples to absorb water and create a gel that slows both digestion and the absorption of sugar into the bloodstream, benefiting dogs with diarrhea or diabetes, or those eating foods made with grain.

Most of the apple's fiber and antioxidants are in the skin, with a serving of apples providing your dog with 70 percent of the antioxidants that carry specific antioxidant, anti-inflammatory, cancer-fighting, and insulin resistance reduction benefits. One antioxidant in apples—quercetin—likes things to move at a leisurely pace: It slows the breakdown of carbohydrates into simple sugars, inhibits allergic symptoms by regulating the release of histamine, regulates genes that help cancer to proliferate, and scavenges for free radicals.

No other fruit or vegetable has more pesticide residue than conventionally grown apples. Since you don't want to throw out the nutrient-packed peel, definitely purchase organic. When shopping for apples to share with your best friend, remember dogs generally prefer the taste of a sweet red apple than a tart green one. Dogs should only be given cored apples, to prevent them from eating the seeds, which contain cyanide in small amounts.

On Your Plate

- Combine a slice of a Pink Lady apple and a slice of Manchego cheese, and wrap it in prosciutto. Broil for 3 to 4 minutes for a fantastic appetizer called Apples on Horseback.

- Julienned apples, beets, carrots, and a dressing of your choice can be combined into a slaw that pairs well with grilled meats.

In the Dog Bowl

- Slice apples and avoid giving the slices skin side up. Many dogs don't like to bite into the skin of fruits and vegetables.

- If your dog is adverse to the skin of an apple, try grating the apple into her food.

KEY NUTRIENTS

Calories 7% • Protein 1% • Total fats 1% • Carbohydrates 29 g • Potassium 11% • B$_6$ (pyridoxine) 12% • C 10 mg per apple • Antioxidants 70%

1 large apple has 110 calories; equivalent to about ⅓ cup of commercial dry food.

Add it to the bowl:

10-lb. dog
⅕ apple

20-lb. dog
⅓ apple

40-lb. dog
⅔ apple

60-lb. dog
¾ apple

80-lb. dog
1 apple

100-lb. dog
1¼ apples

P.B. & A.

I often get asked about peanut butter. It is truly one of my least favorite things to give your dog—full of fat, often with added sugar and preservatives your dog doesn't need. Yet I know your dog enjoys it and you want to share some with him. So, if you're going to feed peanut butter to your best friend, at least do it better with this recipe. Be sure to use peanut butter that does not contain xylitol, which is toxic to dogs.

INGREDIENTS

1 teaspoon peanut butter
½ cup cored, grated apple
Pinch of ground cinnamon

1. Microwave the peanut butter for 30 seconds on high, or until it is melted.

2. Mix in the grated apple and cinnamon and stuff it into a Kong.

3. Store any extra P.B. & A. in the refrigerator for up to 1 day.

Yield: ½ cup

KEY NUTRIENTS:

135 calories per cup • Protein 7% of RDA • Carbohydrate-to-protein ratio 7.3 to 1 • Total fats 26% of RDA • Antioxidants 125% of RDA

Daily allowance:

10-lb. dog
1 tablespoon

20-lb. dog
2 tablespoons

40-lb. dog
3 tablespoons

60-lb. dog
¼ cup

80-lb. dog
⅓ cup

100-lb. dog
½ cup

APRICOTS

In larger litters of puppies, there is usually one runt who may be a bit smaller than others and maybe not as outgoing. But with the right attention, a runt can turn out to be a trustworthy and loving companion. The apricot may very well be the runt of the fruit family. Most often regulated to jams while its larger and juicier brethren, the peach, nectarine, and even the plum, get all the attention, the apricot is just waiting to be discovered and appreciated.

Apricots are most notably high in vitamin A and carotenoids, giving apricots their yellow-orange blush. Combined with a healthy dose of lutein and zeaxanthin, these nutrients will protect your dog's eyes from age-related damage. The vitamin A keeps working as an antioxidant, enhancing immune function, building collagen and ensuring mucous membranes (such as inside the nose) stay moist.

Fresh apricots are generally available during the late summer and dried apricots are a year-round chewy treat. If a fruit being pretty isn't a concern for you, it certainly will not bother your dog, so look for unsulfured dried apricots. Apricot pits contain cyanide, which is toxic, and can cause obstructions if swallowed.

On Your Plate

- Incorporate dried apricots into stuffings for chicken or pork.

- Fresh apricots, pitted and grilled briefly for 3 to 5 minutes, make a great pairing for mozzarella, burrata, or goat cheese.

In the Dog Bowl

- Remove the pit. Chop finely for dogs under 20 pounds, or cut into slices for dogs 20 pounds or larger.

1 apricot has 17 calories; equivalent to about 1 tablespoon of commercial dry food.

Add it to the bowl:

10-lb. dog
¼ apricot

20-lb. dog
¼ apricot

40-lb. dog
½ apricot

60-lb. dog
½ apricot

80-lb. dog
1 apricot

100-lb. dog
1 apricot

- **When roasting meats to add to your dog's meal, add some chopped apricots to enhance their own flavor and soak up the flavor of the meat.**

KEY NUTRIENTS

Calories 1% • Protein 1% • Total fats 1% • Carbohydrates 4 g • Potassium 4% • A 27% • Antioxidants 4%

BANANAS

No sooner do you fill the dog bowl than your dog excitedly starts gulping down the chow. Despite hanging out with humans for 12,000 years, dogs haven't picked up on the habit of chewing every bite 30 times. The canine mouth doesn't secrete the same types of enzymes our mouth does, so the real work begins after a swallow. The stomach is the acidic holding tank where food is combined with enzymes and broken down into components that the body begins to absorb as food enters the small intestine. The pancreas, liver, and gallbladder make their contributions to further break down food, and the absorption of the nutrients really kicks into high gear. When the digested food enters the large intestine, water is reabsorbed, and then there you are with a plastic bag.

The digestive system has so much work to do and bananas are one of the foods that "give back" and say thank you. Bananas contain quickly absorbed glucose and slowly absorbed fructose that provide your dog with energy in two different ways. Bananas have a low glycemic index, beneficial for all dogs, including those with diabetes. Like apples, they are filled with soluble fiber and pectin, which only becomes richer as bananas ripen; this is convenient since it's pretty difficult to get a dog to eat a green banana. The potassium in bananas helps balance the stomach's acid with an alkalizing effect, while other chemicals stimulate the production of the stomach's protective mucus layer. Traveling further through the digestive system, the inulin in bananas feeds the beneficial bacteria in the large intestine.

On Your Plate

- Freeze bananas, peel, and cut into ½-inch slices. Roll in unsweetened cocoa powder or nuts for a delicious and healthy dessert.

In the Dog Bowl

- Yep, you'll need to peel the banana for your dog. Try banana slices mixed into a meal.

- Dried banana chips, without added sugar, are also great training treats.

KEY NUTRIENTS

Calories 3% • Protein 1% • Total fats 1% • Omega-3 (ALA) 8% • Omega 6 (LA) 1% • Carbohydrates 13 g • Potassium 10% • B_6 (pyridoxine) 30% • Antioxidants 5%

1 banana has 105 calories; equivalent to about ⅓ cup of commercial dry food.

Add it to the bowl:

10-lb. dog
1 tablespoon chopped banana

20-lb. dog
⅕ **banana**

40-lb. dog
¼ **banana**

60-lb. dog
⅓ **banana**

80-lb. dog
½ **banana**

100-lb. dog
⅔ **banana**

BANANA GRRRRANOLA BARS

This is the easiest dog cookie recipe you will ever find. Patting it out with wet hands prevents the dough from sticking to your fingers.

INGREDIENTS

3 tablespoons coconut or olive oil, plus more for cookie sheet
3 cups oats
1 ripe banana
¼ teaspoon ground cinnamon
1 to 2 tablespoons water, if needed

1. Preheat the oven to 325°F. Lightly grease a cookie sheet with oil.

2. Pulse the oats in a blender for 30 seconds, or until they are reduced to a fine powder.

3. Add the banana, oil, and cinnamon and pulse for another 30 seconds; the dough should come together in a ball.

4. If the dough is not coming together, add a tablespoon or two of water, and pulse again for 15 seconds.

5. Wet your hands and pat out the dough in an 8-inch square on the prepared cookie sheet. Cut the dough at 1-inch intervals in each direction, using a pizza cutter.

6. Bake the cookies for 30 minutes, or until lightly browned.

Yield: 64 cookies

KEY NUTRIENTS

22 calories per cookie • Protein 6% • Carbohydrate-to-protein ratio 7.6 to 1 •
Total fats 23% • Antioxidants 5%

Daily allowance:

10-lb. dog
1 to 2 cookies

20-lb. dog
3 to 4 cookies

40-lb. dog
4 to 5 cookies

60-lb. dog
5 to 6 cookies

80-lb. dog
6 to 7 cookies

100-lb. dog
8 to 9 cookies

BLACKBERRIES & RASPBERRIES

When we open our doors and hearts to dogs, we offer them shelter in our homes and protect them from the elements. Some dogs will shake off the rain and others live in dread of walking through a puddle. Then there are the fearless dogs who go about their business as if they are wearing the armor of a rhinoceros. Maggie was one such dog who would pursue a tennis ball into a blackberry bush with little regard to thorns. Raleigh and Maggie were the best of friends who chased each other and raced to find dozens of tennis balls. When a foul ball landed in the blackberry

1 tablespoon of blackberries or raspberries has 4 calories; equivalent to about just a few pieces of commercial dry food.

Add it to the bowl:

10-lb. dog
1 teaspoon

20-lb. dog
2 teaspoons

40-lb. dog
1 tablespoon

60-lb. dog
1½ tablespoons

80-lb. dog
2 tablespoons

100-lb. dog
2½ tablespoons

bushes surrounding Maggie's home, Raleigh would wait politely by the edge and defer to Maggie. A bleached blond lab, Maggie would come out with small speckles from the ripest of berries dotted across her body and a few thorns or sometimes a barbed branch hanging from her haunches. For Maggie, all that mattered was getting the ball.

Some dogs may not need our protection from external elements as much as others do, but something all dogs can benefit from is a little internal protection. The pigments responsible for the color in blackberries and the dots on Maggie's fur battle against the mycotoxins often found in alarming amounts of commercial foods. Furthermore, the phytochemicals protect the body from DNA fragmentation, lower the risk of kidney stones, reduce inflammation, defend your dog against cancer, and act as neuroprotective antioxidants.

While you cannot always protect a dog from his own enthusiasm, you can provide a purple tongue that signals antioxidants are acting as armor on the inside of your pet's body.

On Your Plate

- As much as I enjoy blackberries and raspberries, there's an even more delicious berry: the tayberry. They're more difficult to find, but if you find them, stock up and use the same as you would other berries.

- Everybody makes blueberry pancakes; try raspberry pancakes instead! Add the berries just before you flip the pancakes.

In the Dog Bowl

- Crush berries and add to your dog's meal. If he is being persnickety, try crushing the berries and adding some chicken stock to make a light dressing to mix into your pet's food.

- Frozen blackberries and raspberries are a welcome summertime treat when stuffed in a Kong and enjoyed outdoors.

KEY NUTRIENTS

Calories less than 1% • Protein 1% • Total fats 0% • Carbohydrates 2 g •
Manganese 5% • Antioxidants 10% • Low glycemic index

COBBLER IN A KONG

When berries get smashed and I don't want to use them for our desert for aesthetic reasons, I make a cobbler for the dogs. This can be baked in the oven at 350°F for 20 minutes, but I just give it a quick zap in the microwave because I'd rather be out playing in the sun with the dogs.

INGREDIENTS

Coconut or olive oil
1 large egg
6 blackberries, raspberries, or blueberries
¼ cup rolled oats

1. Grease a small baking dish or microwave-safe bowl with a few drops of the oil.

2. In a separate bowl, whisk the eggs with a fork and then add the berries, mashing the fruit against the sides of the bowl.

3. Add the oats and stir to combine. (For a puffier cobbler, you can also grind the oats briefly in a blender before adding to the eggs.)

4. Microwave for 1 minute on HIGH and then allow the cobbler to cool before stuffing it into a Kong.

Yield: ½ cup

KEY NUTRIENTS

240 calories per ½ cup • Protein 29% • Carbohydrate-to-protein ratio 2 to 1 • Total fats 30% • Antioxidants 53%

Add it to the Kong:

10-lb. dog
3 tablespoons

20-lb. dog
3 tablespoons

40-lb. dog
⅓ cup

60-lb. dog
½ cup

80-lb. dog
½ cup

100-lb. dog
⅔ cup

BLUEBERRIES

I never expected to be the victim of a blueberry burglary. When I left a fresh pie pushed back to the far recesses of the countertop, it didn't occur to me that Jackson would eat all eight remaining slices. When I shared our story in *Feed Your Best Friend Better*, readers wrote in to tell me of their own dogs' fondness for blueberries and how they, too, have been burglarized, right at the source—their blueberry bushes. When dogs have such a fondness for blueberries, we might as well go along and buy some extra berries or blueberry bushes just so we can have some.

The trio of phytochemicals providing the deep purple color makes blueberries an anticancer food. Blueberries also increase levels of the neurotransmitter dopamine, which slows cognitive decline, ensuring your dog will remember the flavor for a long time.

The soft powdery blue coating on blueberries is a natural bloom, indicating the berries are fresh. Conventionally grown blueberries contain a high amount of pesticide residues; organic is a better choice.

On Your Plate

- Blueberries pair great with cantaloupe in a fruit salad (both for your plate and in the dog bowl).

In the Dog Bowl

- Split fresh blueberries in half or chop finely before mixing thoroughly into dog food.

- Toss your dog frozen blueberries; often frozen berries will be more likely to be accepted.

KEY NUTRIENTS

Calories 1% • Protein 0% • Total fats 0% • Omega-3 (ALA) 5% • Omega 6 (LA) 0% •
Carbohydrates 3 g • Fiber 2% • Antioxidants 10%

1 tablespoon of fresh or frozen blueberries has 5 calories; equivalent to about just a few pieces of commercial dry food.

Add it to the bowl:

10-lb. dog
1½ teaspoons

20-lb. dog
2 teaspoons

40-lb. dog
1 tablespoon

60-lb. dog
1½ tablespoons

80-lb. dog
2 tablespoons

100-lb. dog
3 tablespoons

BLUE SMOOTHIE

When you serve this to your dog in the morning, let's call it a smoothie. At night we can call it a beneficial blue gravy for his meal.

INGREDIENTS

½ cup blueberries
¼ cup yogurt
¼ teaspoon ground cinnamon
2 tablespoons water

1. Combine all the ingredients in a blender and pulse until smooth.

Yield: ¾ cup

KEY NUTRIENTS

62 calories per ¼ cup • Protein 9% • Carbohydrate-to-protein ratio 2.2 to 1 • Total fats 5% • Antioxidants 35%

Add it to the bowl:

10-lb. dog
2 tablespoons

20-lb. dog
2 tablespoons

40-lb. dog
3 tablespoons

60-lb. dog
¼ cup

80-lb. dog
¼ cup

100-lb. dog
⅓ cup

CANTALOUPE

Maybe it's a coincidence the dog days of summer are at their peak at the same time locally grown cantaloupes are beginning to arrive in the market. When your dog begins panting during the early morning hours and keeps you awake with her restlessness, maybe it's time for some melon. When they are ripe and ice cold, cantaloupes cool your pet down from the inside. Besides being low in calories, a large portion will bring along a surprising amount of nutrients and antioxidants. Vitamin A will keep your dog's immune system, eyes, and mucous membranes healthy, while potassium helps regulate the balance of fluid and electrolytes in her body. Vitamin C is another antioxidant arriving in a healthy amount along with folate to help the body produce glutathione, which will act as a powerful antioxidant.

Cantaloupes contain a lower amount of pesticide residues. Conventionally farmed and organic can both be good choices. Look for heirloom varieties of melons as well to provide similar benefits and amazingly different tastes.

On Your Plate

- The seeds of cantaloupe are often discarded, but they can be roasted like pumpkin seeds. Toast cantaloupe seeds in a skillet over medium heat until they begin to pop, then use them to top a salad.

- Sprinkle cantaloupe with finely ground black pepper to enhance flavor.

In the Dog Bowl

- Cut chunks of cantaloupe away from the rind and add directly to the dog bowl or stuff them in a Kong.

- Frozen chunks of cantaloupe are easy to make cool-down treats without the danger of cracked teeth that can be caused by sharing ice with your dog.

KEY NUTRIENTS

Calories 3% • Protein 3% • Carbohydrates 13 g • Potassium 21% • A 221% • B_9 (folate) 26% • Antioxidants 236%

GRILLED CANTALOUPE WITH YOGURT AND HONEY

When you have the grill going this summer, make a dessert for you to share with your dog. All these ingredients are healthy additions for both you and your four-legged best friend.

INGREDIENTS

½ cantaloupe, cut into quarters
Coconut oil
Greek yogurt
Honey

1. Heat the grill to medium-high, about 400°F.

2. Brush both sides of each cantaloupe wedge with enough coconut oil to cover.

3. Lay the cantaloupe on the grill, cut side down. Cook for 3 minutes, or until grill marks have formed.

4. Flip the cantaloupe over to cook the other side for 2 minutes.

On Your Plate

- Transfer the cantaloupe wedges to a plate and top with a scoop of Greek yogurt and a drizzle of honey. Eat it while it's hot and allow the dog's wedge to cool.

In the Dog Bowl

- Cut the cantaloupe from the rind and cut into bite-size chunks for your dog (see page xv), then a dollop of yogurt and a drizzle of honey.

1 cup of cantaloupe has 55 calories; equivalent to about 3 tablespoons of commercial dry food.

Add it to the bowl:

10-lb. dog
¼ cup

20-lb. dog
⅓ cup

40-lb. dog
⅔ cup

60-lb. dog
¾ cup

80-lb. dog
1 cup

100-lb. dog
1¼ cups

CHERRIES

When you bring a puppy home, it's amazing how fast your new pet grows from an awkward, playful pup into a clumsy adolescent. Then before you know it, your dog is an adult with a unique personality, habits, and preferences. Whereas it takes us a couple of decades to become adults, our canine companions compress their maturation into the span of year, give or take a few months. We can capture a few of the moments with a camera, but pictures and videos can only represent a small percentage of what creates the bond between us and our zoological best friends. Being aware and present, and enjoying the time we have with our dogs throughout their life stages enriches both our lives, but it never seems to be enough time.

Each year I receive a reminder to slow down and appreciate things during the first few weeks of August. I go into the grocery store with the intent to buy some cherries and suddenly they are no longer available. In the reasonable serving sizes for your dog, you'll find that cherries don't provide a significant amount of any particular nutrient in the complete and balanced formula of commercial foods. Well, it's too bad a wider variety of antioxidants isn't part of that formula. The flavonoid phytochemicals that give cherries their deep color are also responsible for their antioxidant, anti-inflammatory, anticancer, and neuroprotective benefits. Anthocyanidins, the class of the flavonoids providing the red tint to cherries, have been found to contain as much antioxidant activity as the same amount of vitamin E. If you happen to miss the season, you can still share some of this healthy fruit with your dog by using frozen or dried fruit, but hopefully you'll find some during the middle of summer.

1 cherry has 4 calories; equivalent to about just a few pieces of commercial dry food.

Add it to the bowl:

10-lb. dog
1 cherry

20-lb. dog
2 cherries

40-lb. dog
3 cherries

60-lb. dog
4 cherries

80-lb. dog
5 cherries

100-lb. dog
6 cherries

Conventionally grown cherries contain a high amount of pesticide residues. Buying organic is highly recommended.

When sharing fresh fruit, be sure to remove both the stem and the pit, which contains cyanide.

KEY NUTRIENTS

Calories 1% • Protein 1% • Total fats 0% • Carbohydrates 5 g • Antioxidants 14%

MANGOES

Blueberries seem like they are the friendliest of fruits. You just give them a rinse and pop them into your mouth or see if your dog can catch one. There aren't any thorns when you're harvesting, no peeling to be done, no stems, and no pits. Mangoes can be just as delicious with their tropical flair, but it's quite reluctant to let go of the giant seed in the middle. I was reluctant to purchase a mango and slice it up myself, until I received a mango pitter. Balancing the fruit on its end and applying one swift push downward left me with two mango halves and the pit in the center. A quick scoop on each side and the fruit was free of the skin as well.

There was a bit of fruit left on the seed and four curious noses in the kitchen, so I grabbed the seed and headed outside. With juice dripping down my hands, I let the dogs practice tearing at the seed with their incisors and each felt determined to carry it off. I held on tightly, not wanting them to also devour the giant seed. By the time we were done, my hands and hounds were sticky with mango juice.

Enzymes in mangoes, similar to the papain in papaya, aid in the breakdown of proteins and are often used to tenderize meat. Mango isn't kind to disease; it's also been shown to be almost as effective as pharmaceuticals at treating giardia. With its vitamins A and C, folate, and a really powerful antioxidant punch, this sticky fruit is worth sticking into both the diet of humans and canines.

1 cup raw mangoes has 99 calories; equivalent to about ⅓ cup of commercial dry food.

Add it to the bowl:

10-lb. dog
2 tablespoons

20-lb. dog
3 tablespoons

40-lb. dog
⅓ cup

60-lb. dog
½ cup

80-lb. dog
½ cup

100-lb. dog
⅔ cup

KEY NUTRIENTS

Calories 3% • Protein 1% • Total fats 1% • Carbohydrates 12 g • A 36% • B$_6$ (pyridoxine) 14% • B$_9$ (folate) 27% • K 12% • Antioxidants 12%

MANGO LASSI

Lassis are a chilled beverage people in India drink to keep cool or to buffer the heat of spicy dishes. Since your dog wears a fur coat even in the summer, he might need a little help cooling off. After mixing this up you can serve it straight in a bowl, use it to top dog food, or freeze inside a Kong for an afternoon treat. As a bonus, your dog is receiving probiotics and enzymes to help with digestion.

INGREDIENTS

½ cup yogurt
½ cup ripe mango, peeled, pitted, and cut into 1-inch pieces
½ cup ice
½ cup water
Pinch of ground cinnamon (optional)

1. Purée all the ingredients in a blender until smooth.

Yield: 2 cups

KEY NUTRIENTS

121 calories per cup • Protein 14% • Carbohydrate-to-protein ratio 3 to 1 • Total fats 8% • Antioxidants 31%

Add it to the bowl:

10-lb. dog
¼ cup

20-lb. dog
⅓ cup

40-lb. dog
½ cup

60-lb. dog
⅔ cup

80-lb. dog
1 cup

100-lb. dog
1⅓ cups

PAPAYA

We hear a lot about the indestructible stomachs of dogs and how they can tolerate more bacteria, larger amounts of meat in their diet, and eating through trash. While this may be true for some dogs, we're finding a larger percentage of dogs have a sensitive stomach, particularly smaller breeds and dogs who have been fed a majority of commercial dry foods their entire life. One food to boost their immune system, enhance digestion, and lower inflammation is the papaya.

Papaya contains the enzymes that break down proteins and assist in digestion. It's a fruit known for alleviating heartburn and preventing stomach ulcers to further soothe the digestive system. The fiber in papaya binds to cancer-causing toxins present in the colon and assists in their elimination due to its high amount of soluble pectin.

Even for dogs with a strong digestive system, including papaya in their diet can give them a nutritional and digestive boost. In addition, papaya also contains healthy doses of vitamins A, C, and folate that act as antioxidants, protect your dog's vision, and maintain both the DNA and health of the cells throughout her body.

Papayas have a lower amount of pesticide residues. Conventionally farmed produce may be acceptable.

On Your Plate

- Replace the tomatoes in your favorite salsa recipe with papaya for a new twist on salsa, perfect with grilled chicken or fish.

- Green papaya contains more papain than ripe papayas do. Try it peeled and grated with a squeeze of lime to replace the lettuce in tacos.

1 cup of raw papaya has 60 calories; equivalent to about 3 tablespoons of commercial dry food

Add it to the bowl:

10-lb. dog
2 tablespoons

20-lb. dog
3 tablespoons

40-lb. dog
⅓ cup

60-lb. dog
½ cup

80-lb. dog
½ cup

100-lb. dog
⅔ cup

In the Dog Bowl

- Remove the seeds and scoop out the flesh of the papaya. Add directly to the dog bowl or stuff into a Kong.

- Combine 1 cup of kefir and 1 cup of papaya in a blender and blend until smooth. Use as a dressing for dog food in the same amounts as for plain papaya.

KEY NUTRIENTS

Calories 2% • Protein 1% • Total fats 1% • Carbohydrates 8 g • A 27% • B_9 (folate) 20% • K 6% • Antioxidants 2%

PEACHES AND NECTARINES

If you've ever spent a summer afternoon with tennis ball–obsessed dogs, you have witnessed the devotion of a hard-training athlete. Incredible leaps catch balls that intended to just sail over a canine nose. Dives, spins, and rolls complete an effort to prevent the ball from ever touching the ground. If you gave the dogs a baseball cap and a whistle, they'd be able to coach a volleyball team and give them some helpful pointers. The athletes most passionate about the sport quickly trot back with a relaxed and happy tail, indicating how pleased they are with their performance. They ball is laid at your feet and it's time for another round. And another. The athletes who play for just the pleasure of the game aren't serious about returning the ball; they'll make you chase them for it. Whichever type of athlete you are playing with, she will demonstrate far more endurance than your arm.

When it's time to put the ball away, why not substitute with something else fuzzy and round? The peach. All the running around will help your dog's weight, as will the phenolic compounds that provide taste, color, and scent of the peach. In both your body and your dog's, these phytochemicals fight inflammation and obesity, particularly metabolic syndrome, which can lead to further diseases.

After a hard day of running around, a (pitted) peach will provide your pet with something that tastes good, is healthy, and helps repair damage brought on by activity. Don't be surprised if she asks for another. And another.

Peaches have a very high amount of pesticide residues. Buying organic is highly recommended.

Both peaches and nectarines should only be given to a dog with the pit removed, as it contains cyanide and could be obstructive if swallowed.

On Your Plate

- Peach Tea: Slice 2 ripe peaches, combine with 2 cups of water, and bring to a boil. Remove from the heat and add a couple of green tea bags. Steep for 5 minutes. Drain (reserving the solids for your dog). Dilute and sweeten to your likeness.

In the Dog Bowl

- Got a bruised nectarine? Don't throw it out; chop it up and throw it in the dog bowl.

- A purée of peaches or nectarines can be frozen and given to your dog in a Kong as a cool-down treat.

KEY NUTRIENTS

Calories 2% • Protein 1% • Total fats 1% • Carbohydrates 7 g • Potassium 7% • A 10% • B$_3$ (niacin) 7% • E 4% • K 7% • Antioxidants 16%

1 cup of peaches has 60 calories; equivalent to about 3 tablespoons of commercial dry food.

Add it to the bowl:

10-lb. dog
2 tablespoons

20-lb. dog
3 tablespoons

40-lb. dog
⅓ cup

60-lb. dog
½ cup

80-lb. dog
½ cup

100-lb. dog
⅔ cup

PEACH OR NECTARINE PARFAIT

With the benefits of fruit and yogurt, this will be sure to be a favorite addition to the dog bowl. Unlike commercial yogurts containing fruit, all the sweetness is going to come from the fruit, not from added sugar. It might even become a favorite for your morning breakfast.

INGREDIENTS

½ cup chopped peaches or nectarines
2 tablespoons blueberries (optional)
½ cup yogurt

1. Stir all the ingredients in a small bowl until all the fruit is coated with yogurt. Mix into your pet's regular meal. Refrigerate any remaining amount in an airtight container for up to 2 days.

Yield: 1 cup

KEY NUTRIENTS

114 calories per cup • Protein 15% • Carbohydrate-to-protein ratio 3 to 1 • Total fats 8% • Antioxidants 38%

Replace 10% of your dog's normal food with the following amounts:

**10-lb. dog
2 to 3 tablespoons**

**20-lb. dog
3 tablespoons to ¼ cup**

**40-lb. dog
¼ to ⅓ cup**

**60-lb. dog
⅓ to ½ cup**

**80-lb. dog
½ to ⅔ cup**

**100-lb. dog
⅔ to ¾ cup**

PEARS

While not quite a nutritional standout like apples, pears still have plenty to offer. First, they're sweet—something that will draw your dog in to the flavor. At the peak of ripeness, they're slightly crunchy, slightly soft. If you bruise one and it no longer tempts you, it's doubtful your dog will feel the same. US households throw between 25 and 40 percent of the foods brought home from the grocery store. Some discards may be due to spoilage, but too often we throw out foods because, in appearance or texture, they have lost their aesthetic appeal to us. Pears ripen quickly, so if you bring home a bunch and you can't keep up with eating them all, consider giving some to your dog as a mix-in to the bowl or in some of the creative ways that follow.

Pears are higher than apples in pectin, but as with apples it's best to include the skin, which is higher in nutrients and antioxidants. When you're peeling pears, particularly if they are organic, send those pear peels into the dog bowl. Pears are considered hypoallergenic for people and it's likely they can offer the same benefits to our canine pals because it is a novel food in their diet.

Pears have a high amount of pesticide residues. Buying organic is highly recommended. As with apples, be sure to core pears before feeding to your dog.

KEY NUTRIENTS

Calories 3% • Total fats 0% • Carbohydrates 14 g • Potassium 5% • B$_9$ (folate) 5% • Antioxidants 6%

1 cup of pears has 80 calories; equivalent to about ¼ cup of commercial dry food.

Add it to the bowl:

10-lb. dog
3 tablespoons

20-lb. dog
¼ cup

40-lb. dog
⅓ cup

60-lb. dog
½ cup

80-lb. dog
⅔ cup

100-lb. dog
¾ cup

PINEAPPLE

If your dog enjoys fruit, give her a bouquet. The pineapple fruit is actually composed of up to 200 flowers joined together around a central core, leaving a sweet, juicy fruit and eyes as the last evidence of the bouquet. Along with the sweet juices, the pineapple delivers a healthy source of manganese that assist the body with thyroid function, energy production, blood sugar control, synthesizing fatty acids, and the formation of bone and tissue. But the real star is the enzyme bromelain, which acts as an antioxidant and helps mediate the immune system's response to inflammation. It's beneficial not only for relieving arthritis pain but also the recovery from sports injuries, making it a great treat after a long hike.

The antioxidants in pineapple are at their peak when very ripe, but so is the sweetness. Pick out pineapples heavy for their size with a sweet smell at the stem. Toxic residues are extremely low in pineapple, so organic or conventionally grown produce can both be good choices. Storing it upside down for a day or two will also help the juices spread throughout the fruit. After it's cut, be sure to use pineapple within the first couple of days, because the quality deteriorates quickly once cut.

KEY NUTRIENTS

Calories 1% • Protein 0% • Total fats 0% • Carbohydrates 5 g • Manganese 15%

1 cup of diced pineapple has 77 calories; equivalent to about ¼ cup of commercial dry food.

Add it to the bowl:

10-lb. dog
1 tablespoon

20-lb. dog
2 tablespoons

40-lb. dog
3 tablespoons

60-lb. dog
¼ cup

80-lb. dog
¼ cup

100-lb. dog
⅓ cup

EAT THIS, DON'T EAT THAT

Both pineapple and spinach have been reported to prevent dogs from ingesting the unmentionable. If your dog does this, you know what I mean. Putting them together in a cookie provides your dog a treat and a healthy dose of discouragement from engaging in unseemly behavior. The core of the pineapple can be used as well, so you don't have to waste anything.

INGREDIENTS

1 cup pineapple chunks

2 cups fresh spinach, or ¼ cup frozen

3 tablespoons olive oil

1½ cups flour (I use spelt flour, but you can use all-purpose, buckwheat, or even rice flour)

2 to 3 tablespoons water (or homemade chicken stock for added flavor)

1. Preheat the oven to 350°F. Line a baking sheet with a silicone mat.

2. In a food processor fitted with a cutting blade, purée the pineapple and spinach to a fine texture by pulsing the mixture 8 to 10 times.

3. Scrape the sides of the bowl, add the olive oil, and give it a few more pulses. Add the flour and process until the dough has a mealy texture.

4. Adding 1 tablespoon of water at a time, process until the dough comes together to form a ball. It may take more or less water, depending on the type of flour used and if you used fresh spinach.

5. Spread out the dough to ¼-inch thickness on the prepared baking sheet, to about 8 inches square. Using a pizza cutter, make seven passes through the dough in each direction, spacing them 1 inch apart.

6. Bake for 30 to 35 minutes, or until dry.

Daily allowance:

10-lb. dog
1 to 2 cookies

20-lb. dog
3 to 4 cookies

40-lb. dog
4 to 5 cookies

60-lb. dog
5 to 6 cookies

80-lb. dog
6 to 8 cookies

100-lb. dog
8 to 10 cookies

7. Store the cookies at room temperature in an airtight container for 3 to 5 days or in the refrigerator for up to a week.

Yield: 64 cookies

KEY NUTRIENTS

20 calories per cookie · Protein 6% · Carbohydrate-to-protein ratio 10 to 1 · Total fats 21% · Antioxidants 5%

PLUMS

Rosemary is supposed to be the food of memory, but for foods that remind me of our dog Baxter, nothing could beat out a plum. I'm not a noisy plum slicer and there was a slight scent of plums in the air, but I didn't think it could be enough to bring Baxter skidding around the corner into the kitchen. The slicing of a plum was more reliable than calling his name or a whistle. Later, when Baxter developed cataracts and could no longer see, he would still rush through the house spurred on by the siren's call of his favorite fruit.

Quite possibly it was one of the phytochemicals in plums sending out a message for Baxter to come running. A single serving of plums contains 78 percent of the antioxidants dogs need per day, including epicatechin, which also served to help Baxter's inflammation, insulin resistance, and glucose tolerance that resulted from his diabetes. In the background, peonidin contributes to the red and purple tint of the plums and fights against cancer and fending off age-related diseases. Too often we reserved this fruit as a treat; looking back I wish we would have included it more often in his diet. Baxter obviously knew something we didn't.

Plums have a high amount of pesticide residues; buying organic is highly recommended. As with other stone fruit, such as peaches, be sure to remove the pit before giving plums to your dog.

KEY NUTRIENTS

Calories 3% • Protein 2% • Total fats 1% • Carbohydrates 13 g • Potassium 9% • A 17% • K 26% • Antioxidants 78%

1 plum has 27 calories; equivalent to about 2 tablespoons of commercial dry food.

Add it to the bowl:

10-lb. dog
½ plum

20-lb. dog
⅔ plum

40-lb. dog
1 plum

60-lb. dog
1½ plums

80-lb. dog
2 plums

100-lb. dog
2½ plums

PLUM & APPLE COOLERS

Many people give their dogs ice cubes to help them cool down and it makes me cringe to think of how dogs can crack their teeth on them. At a cooking demonstration I was giving, an audience member asked for a good alternative and this is what I suggested, because the plums will freeze but the apples will help break up the ice.

INGREDIENTS

6 plums, washed and pitted
1 teaspoon Chicken Liver Cheat (page 44; optional)
1 to 2 tablespoons water (optional)
1 apple, cored and cut into ¼-inch dice

1. Purée the plums and Chicken Liver Cheat (if using) in a blender or food processor. You may need a tablespoon or two of water to do this effectively in the blender.

2. Spread the apples in the ice cube tray and spoon the plum purée on top. Do not pack or it will create a denser cube.

3. Freeze for 4 hours.

4. Serve the cubes by themselves (outside, of course) or in a Kong.

Yield: 12 cubes

KEY NUTRIENTS:

21 calories per cube • Protein 4% of RDA • Carbohydrate-to-protein ratio 20.5 to 1 • Total fats 3% of RDA • Antioxidants 44% of RDA

Daily allowance:

10-lb. dog
1 to 2 cubes

20-lb. dog
3 to 4 cubes

40-lb. dog
4 to 5 cubes

60-lb. dog
5 to 6 cubes

80-lb. dog
6 to 7 cubes

100-lb. dog
7 to 8 cubes

TOMATOES

If you live in a multiple dog household, you probably understand the various personalities living with you and can pretty much figure out who caused trouble while you were out of the house. But when you come home and find somebody has strewn the kitchen garbage across the floor, do you punish the whole pack? Of course not. Tomatoes haven't been so lucky. The green stems, leaves, and even green flesh of tomatoes are toxic to dogs because of their solanine content. Solanine, part of the plant's defense system against pests, can make dogs vomit and cause loose stools, weakness, lethargy, or confusion. Tomatoes' high acid content combined with concerns about solanine caused many people to put every part of the tomato on lists of foods toxic to dogs. However, the amount of solanine present in the fruit is reduced as the tomato matures and develops the red, gold, and orange hues, which also represent an increased amount of lycopene. Lycopene then continues to increase when tomatoes are cooked. There are plenty of reasons to keep your tomato plants where the dog can't get to them, but when yellow and red tomato varieties are at the peak of ripeness, they are certainly okay to share with your dog in moderation.

Tomatoes contain over a dozen different phytochemicals with antioxidant activity and are believed to reduce the risk of neurological and cardiovascular diseases.

KEY NUTRIENTS

Calories 1% • Protein 2% • Total fats 1% • Carbohydrates 5 g • Potassium 9% • Sodium 31% • B6 (pyridoxine) 13% • K 11%

1 cup of tomatoes has 82 calories; equivalent to about ¼ cup of commercial dry food.

Add it to the bowl:

10-lb. dog
2 tablespoons

20-lb. dog
2 tablespoons

40-lb. dog
3 tablespoons

60-lb. dog
¼ cup

80-lb. dog
¼ cup

100-lb. dog
⅓ cup

TOMATO COOKIES

At the end of summer there is a "use 'em or lose 'em" window with tomatoes. This cookie makes the most of your bounty crop and adds a bit of cheese.

INGREDIENTS

3 tablespoons olive oil, plus more for cookie sheet
2 cups oats
1 cup roughly chopped or whole cherry tomatoes
¼ cup basil
⅓ cup grated Cheddar cheese

1. Preheat the oven to 425°F. Lightly grease a cookie sheet with oil.

2. Combine all the ingredients in a clean food processor and pulse until well blended and the dough comes together in a ball, about 1 minute.

3. Turn out the dough onto the prepared cookie sheet. Using wet hands or a spatula, smooth the dough into an 8-inch square. With a pizza cutter or knife, cut into 1-inch strips in both directions.

4. Bake for 15 to 20 minutes, or until dry and toasted.

5. Store the cookies in the refrigerator for up to 5 days or in the freezer for up to 3 months.

Yield: 64 cookies

KEY NUTRIENTS

27 calories per cookie • Protein 16% • Carbohydrate-to-protein ratio 3 to 1 •
Total fats 33%

Serve the following amount as a meal, twice a day:

10-lb. dog
1 cookie

20-lb. dog
2 cookies

40-lb. dog
3 cookies

60-lb. dog
5 cookies

80-lb. dog
8 cookies

100-lb. dog
12 cookies

WATERMELON

Raleigh was always willing to go on a long hike with me; our favorite destinations had a river or lake for her to swim in. With her thick undercoat and dark hair, she appreciated a dip in the water to cool off. Our hikes were often 5 to 7 miles, round-trip. Raleigh would twitch and murmur while napping on the way home, reliving her adventure, while often I would hold a large slice of seedless watermelon for her, to help cool her down from the inside.

Watermelon is most often thought of as a cooling treat and to help replenish fluids; however, it also offers about as many helpful phytochemicals in a slice as it does seeds. Lycopene fights against heart disease and works to reduce oxidative stress on the bones while lutein reduces inflammation, both of which helped Raleigh's posthike recovery. Whether your dog is trying to beat the heat simply from lying in the sun or from a long run or hike, serve this treat ice cold in a generous portion. (Yes, it's okay to freeze it!)

Watermelon has a fair amount of pesticide residues; buying organic is recommended. Remove the flesh from the rind and pick out any seeds, using a fork, to prevent the seeds from causing stomach irritation to your dog.

On Your Plate

- Toast the watermelon seeds just as you would pumpkin seeds and use them as salad topping or snack. They're surprisingly high in protein, magnesium, and B vitamins for their size.

In the Dog Bowl

- Frozen in a Kong with other chopped fruits or vegetables makes a cooling treat that will keep your dog busy.

KEY NUTRIENTS

Calories 3% • Protein 2% • Total fats 1% • Carbohydrates 11 g • Antioxidants 5%

1 cup of watermelon has 46 calories; equivalent to about 3 tablespoons of commercial dry food.

Add it to the bowl:

10-lb. dog
¼ cup

20-lb. dog
⅓ cup

40-lb. dog
⅔ cup

60-lb. dog
¾ cup

80-lb. dog
1 cup

100-lb. dog
1¼ cups

CHAPTER 4

GRAINS, LEGUMES, & SEEDS

The meal recipes provided have a good deal of meat. But meat production takes a heavy toll on our environment and our pocketbooks. When only fed a diet based on meat, a 10-pound dog eating 350 calories per day would consume 100 chickens a year. An 80-pound dog would consume two whole cows per year.

For many people it is impractical to provide a diet completely based upon meat. And that's okay. The recipes presented fulfill your dog's protein requirements, largely based upon meat, but also add vegetables and grains to fulfill your dog's energy needs. Your pet doesn't have a requirement for carbohydrates, but it doesn't mean that she is unable to utilize them. Produce provides calories but only a minute amount of protein and fat. To round out your dog's diet, another option is grains and legumes. Their additional proteins will keep his or her body in full production, plus you'll be providing additional nutrients not present in meat.

Beta-glucans, sugars that occur in plants, are found in higher concentrations in grains and help bolster the immune system, fight cancer, and activate microbial activity in the body. When included in moderate amounts, they can be a beneficial part of your dog's meal. This book offers recipe options that include a moderate amount of grains.

HOW DO DIFFERENT GRAINS AND LEGUMES COMPARE?

Grain/Legume	Carbohydrate-to-protein ratio	Protein completeness	Glycemic index	Calories per cup
Lentils	2 to 1	90%	Low	658
Quinoa	2 to 1	90%	Low	625
Split green peas	2 to 1	90%	Low	672
Garbanzo beans (Chickpeas)	3 to 1	90%	Low	728
Kidney beans	3 to 1	90%	Low	852
Oats	4 to 1	90%	Medium	606
Buckwheat groats	6 to 1	80%	Low	567
Egg noodles	5 to 1	70%	Low	145
Millet	7 to 1	50%	High	756
Barley (hulled or pearled)	8 to 1	50%	Low	704
Brown rice	10 to 1	10%	Low	688
White rice	11 to 1	10%	High	674

GARBANZO BEANS / CHICKPEAS WITH CRUNCH

If there's a legume with an identity crisis, it must be chickpeas . . . or garbanzo beans, as they are also known. And it's not only the name. Give dogs a chickpea and most of them will just spit it out. However, when it's made crunchy, all of a sudden it's deemed a suitable snack. Add some salt, pepper, and 1 teaspoon chili powder if you'd like to make these for yourself.

INGREDIENTS

2 (15-ounce) cans garbanzo beans, drained and rinsed
2 tablespoons coconut or olive oil
½ teaspoon garlic powder
½ teaspoon ground cumin

1. Preheat the oven to 400°F.

2. Shake any excess water from the garbanzo beans and combine in a small bowl with the remaining ingredients. (If you are using coconut oil, melt it first.)

3. Spread the beans evenly on a rimmed baking sheet.

4. Bake for 30 minutes, giving the pan a good shake every 10 minutes. The treats are done when they are dry, lightly browned, and crunchy.

Yield: 1½ cups

KEY NUTRIENTS

474 calories per cup • Protein 15% • Carbohydrate-to-protein ratio 3 to 1 • Total fats 17%

Daily allowance:

10-lb. dog
2 tablespoons

20-lb. dog
3 tablespoons

40-lb. dog
3 tablespoons

60-lb. dog
¼ cup

80-lb. dog
⅓ cup

100-lb. dog
⅓ cup

POPCORN

There are two foods our dog Flynn really flips out for: pizza and popcorn. And when I say flip, I really mean it. As soon as he hears a familiar pop, pop, popitty, popitty, pop he starts jumping across the couch and demonstrating wild acrobatics. Microwave popcorn contains chemicals we're all much better off without; homemade popcorn is just about as easy but also far more delicious. When we have movie night, we reserve some no-salt popcorn for the dogs. I put Flynn's popcorn into a Kong to slow him down a bit and prevent him from breaking his neck when he's jumping around.

INGREDIENTS

Pick a fat: ¼ cup plus 1 to 2 tablespoons olive oil, peanut oil, bacon fat, or coconut oil

⅔ cup popcorn

Pick a seasoning to share:

    3 tablespoons nutritional yeast or grated Parmesan cheese

    ¼ cup chopped fresh parsley, rosemary (avoid rosemary for dogs prone to seizures), or thyme

    ½ cup unsweetened shredded coconut

    1 tablespoon crumbled nori

1. Heat ¼ cup of your preferred fat in a large, deep pot over medium heat.

2. Add a kernel of popcorn, cover, and wait for the popcorn kernel to pop. Add the remaining popcorn kernels and cover again.

3. Keep the pot over the heat but give it a good shake for every 10 pops you hear. As the pops increase, increase the rate at which you shake the pot.

4. Remove from the heat when there is a 2- to 3-second lapse between pops. Give it one more shake, then add your seasoning plus another tablespoon or two of melted fat. Reserve some for your dog, or better yet—place it in a Kong.

5. Add 1½ teaspoons of salt and even a couple of grinds of black pepper to your own popcorn.

Daily allowance:

10-lb. dog
3 tablespoons

20-lb. dog
¼ cup

40-lb. dog
⅓ cup

60-lb. dog
½ cup

80-lb. dog
¾ cup

100-lb. dog
1 cup

SUNFLOWER SEEDS

People often ask about peanut butter. Although in moderate amounts, peanut butter may be safe (note: peanut butter that contains xylitol should not be fed to dogs) and dogs enjoy it in a Kong, it really doesn't have much to offer your dog nutritionally. High in omega-6 fatty acids, total fat content, and sodium, peanut butter just provides things your dog is already receiving in excess.

A better alternative is sunflower seeds. By swapping out the peanut in favor of a seed, you provide your dog with more B vitamins and vitamins E and K, calcium, magnesium, copper, iron, and selenium, with no sugar, 10 percent of the sodium, 30 percent less fat, and 20 percent fewer calories than found in peanut butter.

POSITIVELY BETTER THAN PEANUT BUTTER

This recipe provides your dog with all the nutrients of sunflower seeds, while the fish adds an irresistible flavor and a source of omega-3 fatty acids. The best part is this sticks to the inside of a Kong just like peanut butter.

INGREDIENTS

2 cups raw, sunflower seeds
1 cup dried sardines or other small fish
1 teaspoon ground cinnamon
½ cup water, plus more if needed

1. Process the sunflower seeds for 1 minute in a food processor until it has a fine, meal-like texture.

2. Add the fish and cinnamon and process for another minute.

3. Finally, add the water and blend until smooth and sticky. If desired, add an additional tablespoon of water to increase the stickiness factor.

Yield: 1⅔ cups

KEY NUTRIENTS

Calories 10% • Protein 18% • Total fats 49% • Magnesium 28% • Sodium 4% • Copper 15% • Manganese 21% • B_1 (thiamine) 34% • B_3 (niacin) 34% • B_6 (pyridoxine) 49% • B_9 (folate) 41% • E 56%

1 tablespoon has 24 calories; equivalent to about 2 tablespoons of commercial dry food.

Add it to the bowl:

10-lb. dog
1½ teaspoons

20-lb. dog
2 teaspoons

40-lb. dog
1 tablespoon

60-lb. dog
4 teaspoons

80-lb. dog
2 tablespoons

100-lb. dog
3 tablespoons

CHAPTER 5

HERBS, SPICES, & SUPPLEMENTS

It can take just a pinch or dash of an ingredient to bring out the flavor and add a scent to bring the curious nose of both people and dogs around. Whether it's a sprinkle of cinnamon or a few drops of fish oil, your dog isn't just getting an interesting new taste—you're giving your pet the necessary tools to repair, build and protect his body.

APPLE CIDER VINEGAR

One ingredient receiving far too much credit for its vitamin and mineral content is apple cider vinegar. With only trace amounts of nutrients, the vinegar won't provide significant amounts to make a difference nutritionally. However, the antibacterial properties can help soothe a sore throat, the pectin soothes the digestive system, and it's known to help maintain blood glucose levels. Some people add apple cider vinegar directly to their dog's water dish, but it's more likely you'll have success if you sprinkle the raw, unfiltered type (the kind with the cloudy sediment known as the mother) over your dog's meals.

1 tablespoon of apple cider vinegar has 3 calories; equivalent to about just a few pieces of commercial dry food.

Add it to the bowl:

10-lb. dog
½ teaspoon

20-lb. dog
1 teaspoon

40-lb. dog
2 teaspoons

60-lb. dog
2½ teaspoons

80-lb. dog
1 tablespoon

100-lb. dog
4 teaspoons

CINNAMON

The flavor and scent of cinnamon are powered by cinnamaldehyde, cinnamyl acetate, and cinnamyl alcohol, essential oils also responsible for strong reactions in the body. These essential oils are useful in preventing an overgrowth of *Candida albicans*, a natural and normal yeast in your dog's digestive tract. When this fungus gets out of hand, it travels outside the digestive tract to wreak havoc and cause such symptoms as ear infections, hot spots, digestive upset, and more. Part of the aroma of cinnamon is due to chalcone polymers, phytochemicals that act in the body as anti-inflammatory, antibacterial, antitumor, antifungal, and antioxidant agents. The chalcones also imitate insulin and increase insulin sensitivity in diabetics.

And as a final bonus, cinnamon is also known as a gas reliever, which is why you'll see it added to each of the recipes in this book that includes beans. You can also mix ¼ teaspoon of cinnamon into any meal recipe if your dog tends to be a little on the gassy side.

Ceylon cinnamon is a variety with a slightly sweeter taste and less coumarin, which can be toxic at high doses. As a powerful antioxidant, it doesn't take much cinnamon to have a positive effect, so either the Ceylon or cassia varieties may be used. Just mix it well into any food or treat recipe.

COCONUT OIL

Not all dog breeds are created equal. Since the moment dogs first walked beside us, they have become more specialized into over 300 recognized breeds. We've assisted their development by selecting the traits we desired and nurturing their natural abilities. German shepherds have matured into guard dogs, which grew out of the herding abilities. On the hunt we chose bloodhounds and basset hounds to accompany us for their scenting abilities, whereas greyhounds and Afghans were chosen for their tracking and speed. Today we select the dogs in our home predominately for their companionship, but deep inside they all retain unique and valuable traits.

Today, we're discovering more about oils and the fatty acids that comprise them and learning to value them for their benefits both in our diet and that of our canine companions. Rising in popularity as more research becomes available are the medium-chain triglycerides (MCTs) found in coconut oil. Although they are saturated fats, MCTs are much easier for the body to burn as fuel because they are made of easily absorbed fatty acids. The specific fats found in coconut oil (capric, caprylic, and lauric acid) provide antibacterial, antifungal, antimicrobial, antiviral, anti-inflammatory, and antioxidant activity while also helping the body burn excess calories and promote weight loss. The fats in coconut oil are readily available to the brain, acting as brain food to fuel the special abilities of every dog breed. Coconut oil also helps the body absorb vitamins and minerals, making it an addition that's good from nose to tail.

Look for coconut oil that is not chemically treated (refined, bleached, or deodorized), so the MCTs remain intact.

1 tablespoon of coconut oil has 117 calories; equivalent to about ⅓ cup of commercial dry food.

Add it to the bowl:

10-lb. dog
½ teaspoon

20-lb. dog
1 teaspoon

40-lb. dog
2 teaspoons

60-lb. dog
2½ teaspoons

80-lb. dog
1 tablespoon

100-lb. dog
4 teaspoons

On Your Plate

- Partnering coconut oil with strong flavorings, such as cumin, garlic, or turmeric can help mask the light coconut flavor and provide an antioxidant bonus.

In the Dog Bowl

- A small swipe of coconut oil in a Kong is a better treat for your dog than peanut butter. Go ahead and mix in a pinch of cumin, garlic, or turmeric for your dog as well.

KEY NUTRIENTS

Calories 7% • Total fats 51%

CUMIN

Outside the body, cumin tickles the nose with a charming scent you'll find in dishes throughout the world. Inside the body, cumin stimulates and fortifies the digestive tract, eases nausea, performs as an antiseptic and antibacterial tonic for the blood, inhibits the growth of cancer through antioxidant behavior, and assists in the detoxification of the liver.

Black cumin seed oil, made from black cumin seeds, contains higher amounts of medicinal oils and the omega-3 fatty acid GLA, which reduces inflammation and pain. It is also believed to help fight cancer and allergy symptoms. Supplement as you would with fish oil.

On Your Plate

- When using whole cumin seeds in your own cooking, lightly toast them in a skillet over low heat just until the aroma begins to be released.

- A mixture of ½ cup of honey, ½ cup of orange juice, 1 tablespoon of ground cumin, and 1 tablespoon of freshly ground black pepper makes a great marinade for a roasted chicken.

In the Dog Bowl

- You can add ½ teaspoon of ground cumin or black cumin seed oil to any meal recipe to share the benefits of cumin with your dog.

EGGSHELLS

Most of us either throw out our eggshells or add them to compost, but there's a way to put them to use for your dog. One of the most vital nutrients in your pet's diet is calcium, the most abundant mineral in the body. Ninety-nine percent of that calcium can be found in the bones and teeth, but it's also needed for muscle contraction, nerve impulses, and blood coagulation. Any homemade dog meal would do well to include a teaspoon of calcium in the form of eggshell powder.

EGGSHELL POWDER

Eggshell powder is quick to prepare and uses something you were going to toss in the garbage— instead put it to good use in your dog's body.

As you use eggs, rinse out the eggshells to remove any excess protein. Allow the shells to air dry, then store them in an airtight container until you have enough to make a batch of eggshell powder.

For additional information on eggshell powder, visit me at dogfooddude.com.

INGREDIENTS
12 clean, dry eggshells

1. Preheat the oven to 300°F.

2. Spread the eggshells on a baking sheet and bake for 5 to 7 minutes. This allows the eggshells to dry further, destroys any coating applied by the supplier, kills any harmful bacteria, and makes the shells brittle.

3. Remove from the oven and allow the shells to cool. Process for 1 minute in a food processor or blender until a fine powder is achieved.

Yield: ¾ cup

Add 1 teaspoon to any meal recipe in this book.

KEY NUTRIENTS

1 teaspoon provides approximately 1,800 milligrams of calcium.

FENNEL SEEDS

The slightly sweet licorice flavor of fennel seeds is partly due to an essential oil called anethole, which is incredibly calming on the digestive tract. Adding some ground fennel seeds to your dog's bowl can soothe an upset stomach, heartburn, or cramps by relaxing the muscles of the digestive tract and relieving gas. Like pumpkin seeds, fennel seeds can also fight worms and parasites.

On Your Plate

- Toast fennel seeds over low heat until lightly browned and add to cucumber and tomato salads or just enjoy a small handful after a rich meal to calm your own stomach.

In the Dog Bowl

- Throw a couple of tablespoons of fennel seeds into the pot when making stock. Allow the seeds to steep and release their essential oils into the broth. Strain them out and discard as you would with other solids. Freeze into cubes of broth for when your dog has an upset stomach. This is also a great stock for making rice when your dog doesn't feel well.

You can add ½ teaspoon of ground fennel to any meal recipe.

FISH OIL

Including fish oil in your dog's diet helps reduce inflammation, powers the brain, protects against cancer, and improves the overall condition of your dog's coat and skin. However, there are many different supplements on the market and not all fish oils are the same.

Cod liver oil is very high in vitamins A and D because it is processed from the liver, which stores these vitamins. Dogs with liver disease should not be fed cod liver oil.

The same amount of salmon oil contains almost 200 percent more EPA than cod liver oil and 300 percent of the DHA. Although it is a little more expensive, you get more of the benefits in every teaspoon.

Krill oil is produced from small crustaceans and has about half of the EPA and DHA, but over 300 percent more coenzyme Q10, and is more sustainable.

Both you and your dog could benefit from including more fish oil in your respective diets and one of the easiest ways is through fish oil supplements. If you buy fish oil in capsule form, consider it a daily jellybean for dogs. Avoid giving your pet fish oil "gummies" that contain sweeteners, as the artificial sweetener xylitol is toxic to dogs.

Portion sizes for supplementing commercial foods:

10-lb. dog
1 capsule, every 2 days

20-lb. dog
1 capsule daily

40-lb. dog
1 capsule daily

60-lb. dog
2 capsules daily

80-lb. dog
2 capsules daily

100-lb. dog
3 capsules daily

GARLIC

There is a great deal of information on what foods are dangerous to dogs, and invariably garlic appears on the list next to its cousin, the onion. Holistic veterinarians recommend including a small amount of garlic for its valuable antimicrobial and antibacterial properties provided by the phytochemical allicin and the cancer-fighting power from the coumaric acid it contains. With 50 percent of dogs developing cancer, it's important to get a reasonable amount of garlic in your dog's bowl to help fight against cancer. In addition, garlic can contribute to the prevention of fleas and ticks, not only because it creates a healthier immune system, but also because the little buggers hate it.

The argument against garlic is based on two elements:

🐾 *Guilt by association*: Onions are loaded with thiosulphates, which can cause a condition known as Heinz body anemia, causing your dog's red blood cells to break down. Garlic, on the other hand, has a trace amount of thiosulphates and the amount of garlic used in preparation is far less than one would normally use with onions.

🐾 *The research study*: A study by a Japanese university gave four dogs "1.25 ml of garlic extract/kg of body weight (5 g of whole garlic/kg) intragastrically once a day for 7 days." Since they were given the equivalent of 5 g of whole garlic per kilogram of body weight, the dogs were overdosed on garlic to over 60 times the recommended amount by taking out select components of garlic and injecting it directly into the dogs' stomach.

If your dog was in this experiment, how much garlic would he have been fed?

10-lb. dog
8 cloves per day—over ⅓ pound in a week

20-lb. dog
15 cloves per day—over ⅔ pound in a week

40-lb. dog
30 cloves per day—over 1⅓ pound in a week

60-lb. dog
45 cloves per day—over 2 pounds in a week

80-lb. dog
60 cloves per day—over 2¾ pounds in a week

100-lb. dog
75 cloves per day—over 3½ pounds in a week

I have a chicken recipe (for people only) using 40 cloves of roasted garlic and it's delicious, but it's a dish I only make once a year. I couldn't imagine eating the whole recipe every day for a week, or worse yet, giving the equivalent to my 60-pound dog.

Looking into other foods fed at 60 times the normal amount, I saw one of our dogs' favorite treats, baby carrots, would cause vitamin A toxicity. Eggs are one of the best sources of protein for dogs, but the fat in 60 times the normal amount of eggs would certainly risk causing pancreatitis. Good foods in moderation provide tremendous support to our body, as long as we don't overdo a good thing. However, if you never put them in your body, or your dogs', they can't do their work at all.

The Japanese study confirmed garlic is dangerous, but only if you're taking your dog to a garlic festival. In a reasonable amount, garlic is a safe addition to your dog's bowl, which is why many holistic veterinarians also recommend garlic. However, because garlic comes in many different forms and strengths, I put together this chart to show you how much is safe.

HOW MUCH GARLIC PER DAY IS SAFE FOR MY DOG?

Size Dog	Clove	Chopped	Minced	Garlic Powder	Garlic Flakes	Granulated Garlic
10-pound dog	⅛	⅛ tsp	1/16 tsp	1/64 tsp	1/16 tsp	1/32 tsp
20-pound dog	¼	¼ tsp	⅛ tsp	1/32 tsp	⅛ tsp	1/16 tsp
40-pound dog	½	½ tsp	¼ tsp	1/16 tsp	¼ tsp	⅛ tsp
60-pound dog	¾	¾ tsp	⅜ tsp	3/32 tsp	⅜ tsp	⅕ tsp
80-pound dog	1	1 tsp	½ tsp	⅛ tsp	½ tsp	¼ tsp
100-pound dog	1	1 tsp	½ tsp	⅛ tsp	½ tsp	¼ tsp

When we get down to the smaller dogs, it's just a smidge or sprinkle, but that's all it takes to provide a healthy addition to your dog's chow!

GINGER

When you're spending a sick day at home, medicine will help you feel better physically, but a dog next to your side brings you comfort. When your dog is sick, you can bring your companion comfort by providing him with a little ginger, a food shown to alleviate nausea.

There are plenty of reasons to include fresh ginger in any dog's diet. Ginger contains zingibain, which reduces inflammation and alleviates pain caused by swelling tissue. Heating ginger releases chemicals called gingerols that protect and heal the digestive tract and reduce bloating, gas, and cramps. Because the beneficial volatile oils are concentrated just under the skin, gently scrape away the skin with a spoon, then chop the ginger flesh finely and add to any meal you are cooking.

Fresh, unpeeled ginger can be stored in the refrigerator for up to 3 weeks.

On Your Plate

- For a delicious dressing on a fruit salad, combine 2 tablespoons each of honey, hot water, lemon juice, and grated fresh ginger.

In the Dog Bowl

- Fresh ginger is far superior to its dried counterpart and ½ teaspoon can be incorporated into any meal or treat recipe. If using powdered ginger, use ¼ teaspoon.

1 teaspoon grated fresh ginger has 2 calories; equivalent to about just a few pieces of commercial dry food.

Add it to the bowl:

10-lb. dog
¼ teaspoon

20-lb. dog
½ teaspoon

40-lb. dog
¾ teaspoon

60-lb. dog
1 teaspoon

80-lb. dog
1¼ teaspoons

100-lb. dog
1½ teaspoons

GELATIN

A dog's unique gait can be charming or alarming. Some dogs dance to their own music and others struggle to run. For those dogs suffering from arthritis, inflammation, or old age, a little gelatin might reduce their jiggle. Gelatin is made of collagen, a protein in connective tissue that also allows muscle and skin to retain elasticity. The collagen helps improve the condition of joints, hair, and skin, and can heal a leaky gut. The glycine in gelatin also protects against cognitive decline and seizures. When you are feeding your dog bone broth, you're already providing her with a source of gelatin; otherwise, you can sprinkle unflavored gelatin directly over your dog's food.

KEY NUTRIENTS

Calories 0% • Protein 0% • Total fats 0% • Carbohydrates 2 g

Add it to the bowl:

10-lb. dog
½ teaspoon

20-lb. dog
¾ teaspoon

40-lb. dog
1¼ teaspoons

60-lb. dog
1¾ teaspoons

80-lb. dog
2 teaspoons

100-lb. dog
1 tablespoon

KONG JIGGLERS

Gather up all the Kongs in the house, and give them a good wash before making this recipe. If you don't have enough kongs, your dog will be just as happy having her treat in a bowl.

INGREDIENTS

1 cup chopped carrots, plus additional
1 (¼-ounce) envelope unflavored gelatin
½ cup homemade stock or bone broth (page 25)
½ cup boiling hot water
¼ cup cooked meat (optional)

1. For each Kong you would like to fill, insert the tip of a carrot into the small hole at the end. Cut off the carrot so it is even with the edge of the Kong, then repeat with the remaining Kongs. If necessary, cut the tips off additional carrots to ensure that you have the right size.

2. Chop the remaining carrots until you have one cup. Lightly fill each Kong with pieces of chopped carrot and/or meat and then set it in a glass with the large end pointing up.

3. Pour the stock into a small bowl and then sprinkle the gelatin over the top. Allow the gelatin to soften for 1 minute.

4. Pour the boiling water into the bowl and stir to combine. Allow this mixture to sit for 5 minutes and then spoon into each upright Kong so the Kong is almost filled to the top. Pour any remaining gelatin mixture into ice cube trays and refrigerate.

5. Refrigerate the Kongs, standing in the glasses, for 3 hours and then serve to your dog outside. Store the Kongs and/or any extra gelatin in the refrigerator for up to 5 days.

Yield: 4 large Kongs

Daily Allowance: All dogs—1 filled Kong

KEY NUTRIENTS:

125 calories per Kong • Protein 15% of RDA • Carbohydrate-to-protein ratio 4.2 to 1 • Total fats 5% of RDA • Antioxidants 4% of RDA

HONEY

Seasonal allergies are not fun for anyone, but if your dog is miserable with itching, it's going to make you miserable as well. If your dog is allergic to pollen, you can help desensitize your pet to the allergen by feeding him local honey. The theory is bees carry spores of allergens back to their hive, which are incorporated into the honey. Ingesting these modified allergen spores is supposed to expose the immune system to minute amounts of the allergen and over time reduce the effect of the histamines causing the allergic reaction. It's debated whether this food can help allergies, but I've recommended it to a number of pet owners who were relieved it helped their dogs.

Honey should be raw (unpasteurized and unfiltered) and harvested close to where you live during the time of year where symptoms are present. The proximity to your location increases the likelihood the pollen culprit will make it into your dog's bowl.

Honey is moderately anti-inflammatory, which may also account for some of the allergy relief. A natural amount of peroxide and enzymes provide antibacterial, antioxidant, antifungal, and antimicrobial properties.

While not local for most of us, manuka honey from New Zealand is made from the pollen of the manuka bush. It's so high in antibacterial properties that it has its own grading system called unique manuka factor (UMF). To ensure you are receiving the benefits, be sure to purchase manuka products with a UMF rating of 10 or greater.

KEY NUTRIENTS:

21 calories per teaspoon

1 teaspoon grated fresh ginger has 2 calories; equivalent to about just a few pieces of commercial dry food.

Add it to the bowl:

10-lb. dog
¼ teaspoon

20-lb. dog
½ teaspoon

40-lb. dog
¾ teaspoon

60-lb. dog
1 teaspoon

80-lb. dog
1¼ teaspoons

100-lb. dog
1½ teaspoons

KEFIR

It seems everybody lights up when they see a puppy. Even better than that is a visit with a whole litter of puppies. Yogurt is a great addition to a dog's bowl because it provides friendly bacteria to help the digestive system and support your dog's immune system. However, it's a "one puppy" kind of dairy product, supporting the digestive tract through one or two strains of friendly bacteria. It does a good job, but the body needs a lot more attention. Bring in kefir, a fermented milk or coconut water, and it's like bringing in the litter of puppies—plus a couple more litters to make sure it's a party. With up to 30 different strains of friendly bacteria, kefir can provide whole-body attention.

Kefir acts as a probiotic, much like yogurt, to boost immunity, ease digestive problems, relieve allergies, improve digestion, kill *Candida* and other yeasts, and support detoxification. That's just the first litter of puppies. Kefir can also fight cancer by inhibiting tumor growth.

For lactose intolerant dogs, look for kefir made from coconut water.

KEY NUTRIENTS:

Calories 5% • Protein 2% • Fat 3% • Millions of friendly bacteria

1 tablespoon of kefir has 38 calories; equivalent to 3 tablespoons of commercial dry food.

Add it to the bowl:

10-lb. dog
1 teaspoon

20-lb. dog
2 teaspoons

40-lb. dog
1 tablespoon

60-lb. dog
2 tablespoons

80-lb. dog
2 tablespoons

100-lb. dog
3 tablespoons

KEFIR & TURMERIC

When turmeric is combined with whole milk or coconut kefir, you have an unstoppable duo that will make your dog feel great.

INGREDIENTS
½ cup kefir
1 tablespoon ground turmeric
Pinch of freshly ground black pepper

1. Combine the kefir, turmeric, and pepper in a plastic container fitted with a lid. Give it a good shake to combine and serve in the same amounts as plain kefir.

Yield: ½ cup

KEFIR ICE POPS

1. Freeze plain kefir or Kefir & Turmeric in an ice cube tray until set, about 2 hours. It doesn't have to be completely frozen; in fact, it's even better for your dog's teeth if it isn't. Pop it into a Kong and serve it outside.

PARSLEY

We've all had a dog who wants to give us "a kiss," which is probably a response long left over from their time as puppies. When they were puppies, their mother would lick them to comfort them or to encourage their digestive system to finish its work. You'll often see another dog lick at another dog's mouth as a friendly greeting, which is an act of showing subordination. Some may just be licking at your mouth because they smell what you had for dinner. Whatever the reason, it's a small demonstration of the bond we have with dogs. Unfortunately, dogs aren't really good with their own dental hygiene. An annual visit to the doctor's office not only gives your dog a chance for a physical but also a good dental cleaning. Between cleanings, brushing is an option, but I know few people that actually do it. Providing chew toys and stuffed Kongs to encourage chewing can be helpful as well.

The idea that commercial dry dog foods can help teeth clean is a bit far-fetched. Dogs don't chew their food enough to really make a difference and neither you nor I have a cleaner mouth after chewing on crispy carbohydrates. Parsley won't brush your dog's teeth, but will help provide less offensive kisses.

Parsley doesn't stop at just clean breath. The essential oils in parsley that give it its unique flavor and fragrance act as a mild and harmless irritant to the kidneys, encouraging urine production and detoxification of the body. Parsley also contains phytochemicals with anticancer and anti-inflammation properties. The next time your dog gives you a kiss, it might just be a thank-you for including this healthy ingredient in his diet.

1 tablespoon of fresh parsley has 1 calorie; equivalent to just one piece of commercial dry food.

Add it to the bowl:

10-lb. dog
1 teaspoon

20-lb. dog
2 teaspoons

40-lb. dog
1 tablespoon

60-lb. dog
1½ tablespoons

80-lb. dog
2 tablespoons

100-lb. dog
2½ tablespoons

KEY NUTRIENTS:

Calories 0% • Protein 0% • Total fats 0% • Carbohydrates 0.48 g • A 26% • B_9 (folate) 9% • K 422%

TURMERIC

Turmeric is the Lassie in your spice cabinet. More than any other spice or food, turmeric is an antioxidant hero: Powered by its curcumin content, turmeric outperforms in every situation. Starting from the tip of your dog's ears, it works to eliminate ear infections, improves neurological function, prevents cataracts, lowers the risk of heart disease, detoxifies the liver and improves liver function, regulates stomach acid, promotes digestive health, and eases gastrointestinal disorders. While it's in your dog's body, it fights inflammation, free radicals, cancer, parasites, and diabetes, and speeds healing of wounds. All that before breakfast.

It gets better. Combine turmeric with a small grind of black pepper and the piperine in the pepper increases the effectiveness of turmeric by 2,000 percent. That's like giving Lassie opposable thumbs and a Swiss army knife. Feed turmeric along with coconut oil for better absorption and your dog might just start acting like Lassie, too.

On Your Plate

- Mix ½ teaspoon of turmeric with ½ cup of yogurt, ½ cup of chopped celery, a little freshly ground black pepper, and a cooked chicken breast for a chicken salad.

- Grate fresh turmeric root with a Microplane grater and add to just about anything from salads to mashed potatoes.

In the Dog Bowl

- Add ½ teaspoon of ground turmeric to any meal recipe, to supercharge your dog's health.

- Grate ½ inch of fresh turmeric root into any meal recipe in this book.

YOGURT

In a spoonful of yogurt, millions of beneficial bacteria are waiting to go to work. With just a spoonful, your dog's body receives a workforce dedicated to protecting his body against harmful bacteria and pathogens, manufacturing vitamins, and digesting carbohydrates to turn them into short-chain fatty acids that feed cells in the intestines.

PRE & PRO YOGURT & BANANA

When antibiotics are necessary to help your best friend heal from an illness, the antibiotic doesn't discriminate between beneficial and harmful bacteria; the aim is to eliminate them all. There might have been some harmful bacteria in your dog's digestive tract, but there were also a lot of good bacteria to help maintain heart health and the immune system, and we're also learning some bacteria have an effect on obesity and brain activity. When the prescription regimen is completed, this recipe will help reintroduce beneficial bacteria via the yogurt and feed that bacteria with the soluble fiber in bananas.

INGREDIENTS

½ **banana, sliced**
½ **cup unsweetened, plain yogurt (with live and active cultures)**

1. Mash the banana with a fork and stir in the yogurt. Store in the refrigerator in an airtight container for up to 1 week, or until the expiration date on the yogurt container—whichever comes first.

2. This can also be frozen in ice cube trays for 2 hours to create a soft frozen treat.

Yield: 1 cup

KEY NUTRIENTS

8 calories per tablespoon • Protein 2% • Carbohydrate-to-protein ratio 3.7 to 1 • Total fats 1%

Add it to the bowl:*

10-lb. dog
1½ teaspoons

20-lb. dog
2 teaspoons

40-lb. dog
4 teaspoons

60-lb. dog
1½ tablespoons

80-lb. dog
2 tablespoons

100-lb. dog
2½ tablespoons

*If your dog is just getting over an illness, start out with half of the above amount for the first couple of days.

CHAPTER 6

FOODS FOR SPECIFIC AILMENTS

Some of the best medicine is food. Food not only nourishes the body, it also provides you a means of expressing your affection when your dog doesn't feel all that well. The meals throughout this book are simple, and certain combinations of food either provide or withhold specific nutrients and can help dogs with a variety of conditions. In most cases, I recommend adding a vitamin and mineral supplement to keep your dog working toward a return to top form. With allergies, gastrointestinal issues, and liver disease, it's best to consult with your veterinarian to determine when supplements are right for your dog.

ALLERGIES

While avoiding allergens is the most important aspect of allergy treatment, there are a few foods to relieve the itching and redness. Probiotics in yogurt or kefir along with the prebiotics in apples, bananas, and asparagus can help to boost the immune system and inhibit harmful yeast and bacteria. Honey can also help relieve seasonal environmental allergy symptoms. To reduce inflammation, be sure to add fish and turmeric to the diet.

This book offers many foods and meals for you to choose from and, of course, you can always substitute if you know a particular food is an allergen. Nutriscan testing (visit nutriscan.org) can help define the foods that cause sensitivities in your pet.

Recommended Recipes

- Lamb Hash, p. 63

- Lamb & Lentils, p. 68

- Pork & Applesauce, p. 71

- Salmon Hash, p. 88

ARTHRITIS

When old age and stiffness sneak up on your pet, sneak in supplements for relief: fish oil, glucosamine, MSM (methylsulfonylmethane), or green-lipped mussel extract. Diet composition can have a large impact on the arthritis pain when meals are composed of fish, beef, ginger, squash, green beans, kale, and broccoli. Feel free to add cinnamon, garlic, ginger, turmeric, and gelatin to meals to provide further anti-inflammation benefits.

Recommended Recipes

- Buttered Up with Beef, p. 11

- Gingered Beef & Broccoli, p. 12

- Beef & 3 Cs Casserole, p. 17

- Simply Beef & Yam, p. 22

- Mackerel Mix-In, p. 82

- Salmon & Veg, p. 87

CANDIDIASIS

Normally *Candida albicans*, a fungal yeast naturally occurring in your dog's body, goes about its business as an upstanding member of the flora in the intestines. When a serious wound occurs or the body's pH balance is thrown off, *Candida* makes a break for it and terrorizes the body. Symptoms can occur anywhere in the body from the tip of the ears to right where the tail starts. To restore the immune system, it is important to put *Candida* back in its place, which most often starts with a prescription regimen from your veterinarian. To support and help restore order in your dog's body, also include foods with antifungal properties: cabbage, cinnamon, coconut oil, coconut meat, garlic, parsley, parsnips, and ground pumpkin seeds.

Recommended Recipes

- Moroccan for Mutts (add parsley), p. 49
- What's Bubbling, p. 106
- All the Guts and All the Glory (Pumpkin), p. 131
- Kefir & Turmeric, p. 204

CANCER

A high-fat, high-protein diet with fewer carbohydrates is preferred for dogs who are fighting cancer. On the plus side, this means your dog is going to have a great meal filled with meat. Additionally, we want to include fish and low-carb vegetables full of antioxidants, to repair DNA and prevent tumors. Meat from grass-fed animals is preferred, due to the higher amount of conjugated linoleic acid (CLA), which helps kill cancer cells. In each of these meals, ½ teaspoon of ground turmeric would be another good additive.

Recommended Recipes

- Gingered Beef & Broccoli, p. 12
- Not Too Chili for Kale, p. 21
- Chicken Thighs, Squash, & Sprouts, p. 50
- Ad Hoc Lamb Stew, p. 66
- Lamb & Lentils, p. 68
- Mackerel Mix-In, p. 82
- Salmon & Veg, p. 87

DEGENERATIVE MYELOPATHY

A diet low in saturated fats can slow the progression of degenerative myelopathy (DM) in dogs, a spinal cord disease that is much like multiple sclerosis in humans. Important for dogs with DM is to have a good source of protein to retain as much muscle tone as possible, as well as foods that are gluten-free to reduce inflammation and high in such antioxidants as quercertin, fisetin, ferulic acid, and kaempferol, which have neuroprotective benefits and help in the production of neurotransmitters.

These recipes are dedicated to our neighbor Scout, the bravest dog on two wheels.

Recommended Recipes

- Chunks of Chuck, Rice, & Veggies, p. 20
- Cluck & Quinoa, Too, p. 31
- Quick Chicken & Oats, p. 51
- Lean Turkey & Lentils, p. 57
- Salmon & Veg, p. 87

DIABETES

Slow-digesting foods with plenty of soluble fiber provide diabetics a more regular blood sugar level. You want to be sure to include lentils, yams, cinnamon, kale, turkey, and garlic for their phytochemicals that assist in maintaining blood glucose levels and insulin sensitivity. Both cherries and asparagus help increase insulin production and can be added to any of these meals.

Recommended Recipes

- Not Too Chili for Kale, p. 21
- Cluck & Quinoa, Too, p. 31
- Gizzard Grind, p. 38
- Quick Turkey Quinoa, p. 58
- Turkey, Yam, & Kale, p. 59
- Lamb & Lentils, p. 68

EYE HEALTH

Vitamin C, carotenes, and the cataract-preventing twins lutein and zeaxanthin are an important part of keeping a dog's eyes healthy and focused on giving you that adoring look. In addition, omega-3 fatty acids help reduce the risk of cataracts and retinal damage. Many of the recipes include apples, red bell peppers, carrots, butternut squash, and pumpkin for these nutrients. A half-teaspoon of turmeric can be added to any of the recipes (where it is not already specified) for additional help in preventing cataracts.

Recommended Recipes

- Chicken Breast & Veggies, p. 32

- Chicken Thighs, Squash, & Sprouts, p. 50

- P.O.P.S. (Pork, Oats, Pumpkin, & Spinach), p. 73

- Mackerel Mix-In—Meal Topper (added to any meal), p. 82

GASTROINTESTINAL

To get a dog with a defective digestive system back on track, the first couple of days should just be well-cooked rice with a little chicken. Days three and four can start light foods, and adding canned pumpkin or banana to your pet's meal can help bind the stool and replace electrolytes. Apples, pears, ginger, gelatin, and blueberries can help alleviate the diarrhea, while green beans, kale, parsley, and spinach replace the vitamin K the body had trouble producing while a dog had diarrhea.

If your dog is suffering from heartburn, papaya can help put out the fire.

Recommended Recipes

- Cluck & Quinoa, Too, p. 31

- Chicken Breast & Veggies, p. 32

- Pre & Pro Yogurt & Banana, p. 208

GIARDIA

Dogs with giardia, a protozoan infection, need to be brought back into balance by using the aforementioned gastro-intestinal suggestions, but in the long term, the best meal to fight giardia is Dessert for Dinner. This meal contains blueberries to help firm up the stool, mangoes to fight the giardia, and a low amount of fat to ensure your dog's stomach is not upset by added fat.

Recommended Recipe

- **Dessert for Dinner, p. 30**

GLUTEN SENSITIVITIES

All the recipes in this book are gluten-free, provided any grains you use are produced in gluten-free facilities. Since many of the meals are grain-free, you shouldn't have to worry about gluten at all.

Recommended Recipes

- **Moroccan for Mutts, p. 49**
- **Lamb & Lentils, p. 68**
- **Lean Turkey & Lentils, p. 57**

HEART DISEASE

For dogs with heart disease, sodium should be kept low, right near the RDA. Potassium and magnesium are essential to help maintain a balance of fluids and to keep chemical reactions in the body functioning. Such foods as bananas can help stock up the potassium, while ground pumpkin seeds and spinach can be added to the bowl to help your dog get enough magnesium.

Recommended Recipes:

- **Stolen Roast, p. 19**

- **Cluck & Quinoa, Too, p. 31**

- **Ground Chicken, Pears, and Quinoa, p. 53**

KIDNEY DISEASE

Prescription diets for kidney disease are some of the most unappealing foods to dogs. Usually high in grain and corn gluten meal, it's no wonder many dogs just turn their nose up at them. A moderate amount of protein, magnesium, phosphorus, vitamin D, and reduced sodium are called for, while B vitamins, omega-3 fatty acids, potassium, and zinc should be increased.

Recommended Recipe

- **Lamb Hash with sardines added, p. 63**

KIDNEY STONES

It's important to know the type of kidney stone your dog has been building up, to know what types of diet changes are necessary. Struvite crystals are the result of an infection, which needs to be treated, but no additional diet changes are required.

Prevention of calcium oxalate stones requires a diet containing low or moderate amounts of oxalic acid and high in magnesium and vitamin B_6 (pyridoxine). Protein should be kept at moderate, but not in restricted amounts. The high amount of proanthocyanidin compounds found in high amounts in blackberries and apples can lower the risk of kidney stones, making both of these foods a welcome addition to any recipe.

♣ *Very low-oxalate foods*: asparagus, Brussels sprouts, cabbage, cantaloupe, cauliflower, cherries, coconut, cranberries, eggs, fish, garlic, lettuce, nectarines, papayas, peaches, peas, pineapple, plums, pumpkin, watermelon, wild rice, yogurt, and zucchini.

♣ *Low-oxalate foods*: apples, apricots (fresh), bananas, beef, broccoli, chicken, garbanzos, lentils, mackerel, pears, red peppers, pumpkin seeds, raspberries, salmon, and sunflower seeds.

♣ *Moderate-oxalate foods*: blackberries, blueberries, brown rice, carrots, celery, green beans, mangoes, oats, potatoes, rutabagas, tomatoes, and winter squashes.

♣ *High-oxalate foods*: beans, dried apricots, figs, kiwi, deep green leafy vegetables, okra, peanut butter, potatoes, sweet potatoes, and tomato paste.

Recommended Recipes

- Stolen Roast, p. 19

- Ad Hoc Lamb Stew (choose very low- and low-oxalate foods), p. 66

LIVER DISEASE

Avoiding red meat, excess sodium, and copper and reducing the amount of protein a dog eats is important with liver disease. It's beneficial to have protein come from grains rather than animal sources and to keep vitamin A close to the RDA.

Recommended Recipe

- Ground Chicken, Pears, & Quinoa, page 53, with following modified amounts:

  3 cups chicken stock or bone broth (page 25)
  ½ pound ground chicken
  1 cup uncooked quinoa
  1 cup chopped green beans
  1 red Anjou pear, cored and stemmed

MENTAL HEALTH

As puppies, dogs need the omega-3 fatty acids DHA and EPA to build a healthy noggin and to ensure all those puppy-training classes are remembered. Throughout their lives, fish and fish oil are important components in their diet to keep them healthy and to nourish their brain. In addition to fish, apples, blueberries, and plums all contain antioxidants that protect the health of neurons in the brain.

Recommended Recipes

- Mackerel Mix-In—Meal Topper, p. 82
- Salmon & Veg, p. 87

OBESITY

It's time for a check-in. Does your dog have an hourglass shape when viewed from above, look straight, . . . or bulge out a bit? Can you easily feel your pet's ribs or is there a little bit of extra padding? Ideally your dog would have a bit of an indent when viewed from above and the ribs would be easily felt. If your dog needs to lose a few pounds, I've got good news: Every recipe in this book is lower in calories than commercial dog food. Take your pick, and your dog will still have a full belly and lose a bit of weight even when fed the same amount.

Recommended Recipes

- All

POSTSURGERY OR INJURY

The trauma of surgery and the pain of recovery take a toll on dogs and it's distressing for those of us who share their lives. Dogs going in feeling not so great get knocked out, and then wake up in more pain, more confused than they were before. In a few weeks your dog will feel better, but he can't comprehend that the bizarre and painful experience is actually a healing process, enabled by the dedicated and compassionate care from veterinary surgeons and their staff. After you've thanked the doctors, it's time to take your pet home and get to the work of helping him heal. Nutrients essential for the healing of wounds include arginine, vitamin C, zinc, omega-3 and omega-6 fatty acids, and antioxidants. Nothing says "get well soon" like a homemade meal.

Recommended Recipes

- **Not Too Chili for Kale, p. 21**

- **Chicken & Vegetables, p. 52**

- **Mackerel Mix-In—Meal Topper, p. 82**

- **Shards of Spears, p. 98**

- **Pre & Pro Yogurt & Banana (after a course of antibiotics is finished), p. 208**

SKIN HEALTH

Wearing a fur coat through every season has to get itchy every now and then. When your dog's skin and coat turn for the worst, many people attribute it to an undiagnosed allergy. In actuality your dog might just need a taste of the sea. Omega-3 fatty acids can not only help with inflammation, but actually improve the overall condition of your pet's coat and skin. In addition to fish, make sure your dog has healthy gut bacteria by feeding her a little yogurt, because good health starts from the inside out.

Recommended Recipes

- Mackerel Mix-In—Meal Topper, p. 82

- Salmon Sauce, p. 86

- Salmon & Veg, p. 87

- Salmon Hash, p. 88

- Pre & Pro Yogurt & Banana (after a course of antibiotics is finished), p. 208

CHAPTER 7

FOODS TO AVOID
(EVEN IF THEY BEG)

Part of what inspired me to write this book was the list of foods often published online or in magazines about the foods you shouldn't give your dogs. Invariably, some of the misconceptions about different foods sneak onto the lists. Instead of focusing on what's not possible, my intention is to focus on what foods are beneficial and why. For such foods as bacon and peanut butter that I'd rather not have you feeding your dog, I've shared some tips with you on ways you can give in and provide a safe amount. However, some foods still remain forbidden, so let's do a quick wrap-up.

🐾 *Alcoholic beverages* have a stronger effect on your dog than they do on you, so keep your glasses up high.

🐾 *Avocados*—the leaves, skin, and pits of avocados as well as the flesh of certain types of varieties are toxic to dogs. Although avocados contain beneficial fats, there are better sources like fish that don't have potential negative side effects.

🐾 *Caffeine*—coffee, tea, and soft drinks can affect your pet's nervous system and heart.

🐾 *Chocolate* contains caffeine, theobromine, and theophylline, which effects your pet's nervous system, heart, and kidneys. If your dog gets into the Halloween candy, call your veterinarian immediately.

🐾 *Fruit pits and seeds* can cause blockages in your dog's throat or digestive system and contain a small amount of cyanide.

🐾 *Grapes and raisins* contain an unknown toxin damaging to kidneys.

🐾 *Hops*: Gardeners and home brewers beware—your fresh or spent hops are toxic to dogs and may result in vomiting, seizures, or death.

🐾 *Macadamia nuts* affect both the nervous and digestive systems and may cause lethargy, vomiting, muscle tremors, joint pain, or seizures.

🐾 *Nutmeg and mace* can excite the central nervous system, causing vomiting or seizures.

🐾 *Onions* contain a high amount of thiosulphates, which damage red blood cells. Although the amount in store-bought stocks is minute, it's not worth chancing it. Also avoid feeding baby foods to your dog because onion powder is often an ingredient.

🐾 *Raw salmon and trout,* particularly from the Pacific Northwest, contain a parasite responsible for severe symptoms and even death.

🐾 *Turkey fat and skin,* or as I call it the Thanksgiving Bomb, is known to cause pancreatitis flare-ups. The same thing goes for the fatty trim off a steak.

🐾 *Xylitol* is a sweetener used in some brands of peanut butter and many sugar-free gums, baked goods, and toothpastes. In your dog, xylitol increases the production of insulin, rapidly lowering blood sugar levels to dangerous levels, leading to seizures and liver failure, which can be fatal.

If you notice your dog panting excessively, drooling, shaking, disoriented, having seizures, muscle tremors, or vomiting, call your veterinarian immediately.

RESOURCES

This book is the result of research that took me through 50 books and 100 scholarly articles. There is a lot of information and misinformation on the Internet; if you would like to learn more about nutrition for you or your pet, I recommend the following trusted resources:

dogaware.com—My colleague Mary Strauss has been analyzing and reviewing recipes for Whole Dog Journal for years and has been an invaluable source of information. Mary has many articles on her website that provide information on specific ailments. This site is worthy of a bookmark.

drjeandoddspethealthresource.tumblr.com—Dr. Dodds unknowingly has been my online mentor. Her articles cover a wide variety of pet health and nutrition topics. Her book *Canine Nutrigenomics* is a must-read if you want to learn more about pet nutrition. Dr. Dodds also owns hemopet.com and nutriscan.org, resources for learning more about what is going on inside your dog's body.

rodneyhabib.com—If you want a chuckle while learning something about pet nutrition, check out Rodney's articles and clever illustrations. Rodney is a frequent contributor to *Dogs Naturally Magazine* and host of the Raw Round Up, an online conference about raw food for dogs.

In researching nutrition, a number of books were helpful. I apologize to the Multnomah County Library for the many overdue notices I have received, but I just couldn't part with these books. I have gladly paid my late fines to support your wonderful facilities and staff.

Collins, Elise Marie. *An A–Z Guide to Healing Foods: A Shopper's Reference.* Conari Press, 2010.

Grotto, David. *The Best Things You Can Eat.* Da Capo Lifelong Books, 2010.

Dodds, Dr. Jean, and Diana R. Laverdure. *Canine Nutrigenomics: The New Science of Feeding Your Dog for Optimum Health.* Direct Book Service, 2015.

Murray, Michael T., Joseph Pizzorno, and Lara Pizzorno. *Encyclopedia of Healing Foods.* Atria Books, 2005. (One of my favorite books!)

National Geographic Complete Guide to Natural Home Remedies: 1,025 Easy Ways to Live Longer, Feel Better, and Enrich Your Life. National Geographic, 2014.

Pinnock, Dale. *Healing Foods: Prevent and Treat Common Illnesses with Fruits, Vegetables, Herbs, and More.* Skyhorse Publishing, 2011.

Price, Joanna McMillan, and Judy Davie. *101 Healthiest Foods: A Quick and Easy Guide to the Fruits, Vegetables, Carbs and Proteins That Can Save Your Life.* Ulysses Press, 2009.

Thomas, Cathy. *50 Best Plants on the Planet: The Most Nutrient-Dense Fruits and Vegetables, in 150 Delicious Recipes.* Chronicle Books, 2009.

For more information on calories, specific nutrients, picking out a commercial food, and specifics about feeding dogs with serious ailments, please check out my first book, *Feed Your Best Friend Better* (Andrews McMeel, 2012).

ACKNOWLEDGMENTS

Dan Crissman

Even as my word count continued to climb you were rooting me on to include more pairings. Thank you for your guidance, enthusiasm, and endless supply of patience. I'm so pleased that we were *paired* together on this project.

Salty

From making dinner because I was too exhausted after recipe testing to ensuring we went away on vacations with and without the dogs, you provide me with balance. How many times did you say, "Is there anything else to eat in this house other than dog food?" And then you would make delicious dinners out of the scraps left from recipe testing. Next time I'm in the kitchen, it will be cooking for you so you can finish your book. Mucho.

Jane Crist

Mom, as a child I spent my early evening hours watching you prepare our meals. Sunday nights were my favorite because you went all out with roasts, mashed potatoes, and popovers. We talked while you chopped or sometimes you asked me to read to you. The conversations and jokes were as important to my development as the delicious meal, and formed my passion for both the written word and good food. Thank you for your endless energy, note taking, monitoring of pencils and kitchen towels, and laughter as we tested recipe after recipe.

Our Pack (Flynn, Frank, & Duncan)

The three of you make me laugh and remember to play more often. My study breaks with you kept me going and your taste-testing each recipe is much appreciated. With this book finished, it's time I get to work on our backlog of walks.

Patti Harrison

Your kitchen has often been a respite from my own. I am truly amazed at the meals you create and the cocktails you shake. For over a decade we have been cooking together, always with our combined pack of dogs underfoot. Thank you for your enthusiasm, friendship, and being an important part of our family. I enjoy food more in your company.

The J's: Joan & Jerry

Now you know why I was holed up for three solid months. We met at the book launch for my first book and I was immediately enamored with the adventurous, funny, intelligent, and incredibly supportive duo you are. Our friendship is one of the best things to develop from the experience of writing FBYFB.

Jennifer Bush

I wish you lived in town so we could cook together and get in more trouble. Thank you for your suggestions to make this a better book.

Michelle Brenes

"Everybody has to eat." Our dinner out helped me further define much of what I intended to do and initiated many rewrites. You nudged me down this path almost a decade ago and I'm thankful you did.

Annie Mitchell & FP&A team at Adidas

"I'll be out of the office on Monday" was a familiar phrase during the last few months of writing this book. Thank you for your flexibility and support. I enjoy being part of your team at Adidas and admire you both for your wisdom, hearty laughs, and determined work ethics.

Sally Ekus

I am blessed to have you as an agent and as a friend. The Lisa Ekus Group has been an incredible partner in all my endeavors. Please come to Portland; we have great tacos.

Rodney Habib

My brother in nutrition, you are an amazing presenter and your passion inspires not just pet owners, but also those of us so dedicated to pet nutrition. When we ran out of options with Raleigh, your suggestions made her last months more comfortable. Thank you for making me laugh while also broadening the scope of how we can help our pets.

Dr. Jean Dodds & Diana Laverdure

I purchased *Canine Nutrigenomics* just as I was going into full writing mode and found it to be one of the best-researched and -documented books on canine nutrition. I read your book over the course of two days and referred to it often over the last few months. It is my hope I present the "how to" of dog nutrition in a way that makes you proud. A special thanks to Diana, the Pet Food Diva; your detailed feedback was especially helpful.

Mary Strauss

Meeting with you and "nerding out" over the details of canine nutrition was truly a highlight of my adventures with *Feed Your Best Friend Better*. Thank you for your time not only in answering my questions but also in capturing so much important knowledge and being so willing to share your expertise.

Genevieve Smith, Kristi Brokaw & Heather Sweeney

Thank you for the review of my early drafts and your thoughtful feedback. As you read through the final work, I hope you see where you made a difference.

INDEX